ROCK BOTTOM AND BACK™

From Desperation to Inspiration

Susan Mustafa
with Earl B. Heard

FIRST EDITION

Cover design by Heather Cavalier

Library of Congress Control Number: 2016910562

CPSIA Code: PBANG0816A
Hardback ISBN-13: 978-1-63177-454-6
Paperback ISBN-13: 978-1-63177-924-4

This book is dedicated to our loving and forgiving God, who has given those we have featured here the strength to overcome unimaginable adversity and the courage to become shining examples to others. It is also dedicated to Margie and Leo Heard and John and Yvonne Bodi, who have helped me, my family, and BIC Alliance come back from rock bottom many times.

Earl B. Heard

CONTENTS

MORE ROCK BOTTOM AND BACK HEROES 141

INTRODUCTION

Throughout my life, I have hit rock bottom several times—personally, professionally, and spiritually. There were times when I couldn't see a light at the end of the tunnel, but I knew I couldn't give in or give up. During those times, I always thought about my father, who began suffering with severely impaired vision when I was a junior in high school, and as a result was laid off at the plant where he worked. With little hope of finding employment, he didn't give up. Not once did I hear him complain about his lot in life. Instead, he found a way to open a small coffee shop and became more successful and more at peace as a blind man than he had been when he had sight. He has always served as an inspiration to me to stay upbeat and keep fighting, no matter what the circumstances of my life might be.

Rock bottom can come in many different forms. Sometimes intense trauma can lead us to make bad decisions that soon compound one upon another. Sometimes we are just out to have a good time and suddenly find ourselves addicted to alcohol, drugs, gambling, or sex. Other times, things that happened in our childhoods come back to haunt us with a vengeance, causing us to act in ways we would have never thought possible. And sometimes the loss of a loved one can cause us to experience grief so profound that we have difficulty functioning.

Many of us have hit rock bottom, or we have friends or family members who have struggled to cope with trauma, addictions, and pain. Rather than pass judgment, it is always important to understand the events that pave the way to rock bottom. How you bounce back is what's important. The people we have chosen to feature in this book came back against incredible odds and then used their experiences to help others.

Many years ago, I bought a case of books from Dr. Joseph Jacobs, the founder of Jacobs Engineering Group. At the time, I didn't have two nickels to rub together, but I thought if I showed interest in the book he had written, I could get his business and give the books as gifts to my clients. What surprised me was that I developed many great business relationships through those books. It was then that I realized how powerful books could be, not only for learning and reading enjoyment, but also for sharing knowledge and inspiration with others. I started buying inspirational books and giving them away, secretly hoping to one day create my own. In 2005, I launched BIC Media Solutions and began my quest to help others through books designed to improve the lives of those who read them.

Rock Bottom and Back is my effort to provide inspiration, faith, and hope through real-life experiences of people who have gone from successful lives to the bottom of the barrel and back again. I knew that this book had great potential when we started, but I had no idea how powerful these stories would be until the book began taking shape. Through the process of creating our companion DVD—a film that features inspiring interviews with some of the people in this book—we formed a partnership with the New Orleans Mission. I'm so proud to say that the homeless people at the mission learned new job skills through their participation in the filming. Before this book was completed, it was already serving as a tool to help others. While it began as a way to provide hope, it has turned into one of the greatest blessings of my life.

So many times, I have been on the brink of desperation. I know what it's like to lose everything. Many people helped me find my way back, and my hope is that this book and the incredible stories of the people chronicled here will help those who feel that same desperation to understand that they are not alone. Hope is just a prayer away. Help is available. All you have to do is reach out your hand. And when you get back on top of the mountain, remember how you got there and reach out your hand to someone else.

Together, we can change the world.

Earl B. Heard

When Earl Heard approached me about writing this book, I knew immediately that it would be a meaningful project. Earl and I had a long history, which began when he gave an aspiring writer a chance and hired me as an editor at BIC Alliance. At the time, I had recently divorced, moved to a new city, and started my life over. Back then, I had no idea that I would one day write true crime books and spend my life investigating the very worst in human nature.

Because I live in the dark world of serial killers, I always try to write something inspirational at the same time I am writing a true crime book, which helps to keep my emotional well-being intact. I've found that when one lives in darkness all the time, depression and fear can replace what is normally a healthy outlook on life.

When I began to work on this project, I was happy that I would be able to write a book about some incredible people who believed in sharing their blessings. I had no idea how deeply I would be affected by the lives of the people I interviewed. I learned so much about addiction, abuse, homelessness, sex trafficking, trauma, loss, and then healing and recovery. These people come from all walks of life. They each have different reasons for hitting rock bottom, and they each worked diligently on their recovery. But then an amazing thing happened. They all used their experiences to change the lives of people they didn't even know.

There are twenty-two people featured in this book. Each one of them has helped improve the lives of hundreds of people—disabled children, alcoholics, drug addicts, addicted gamblers, the homeless, sex-trafficked young women, those suffering with trauma-related depression. Through their stories, I learned that one person truly can make a difference.

My hope is that those who read this book will pass it along to someone else, and that each person who reads it will take a close look at their own lives, count their blessings, and then use those blessings to help someone else. For those who are currently at rock bottom, please remember that when darkness surrounds you, if you search hard enough, you will find a light.

Run toward it.

A hand will be there to pull you to safety.

Susan Mustafa

DR. BOBBY SMITH

Blinded state trooper shares vision of hope

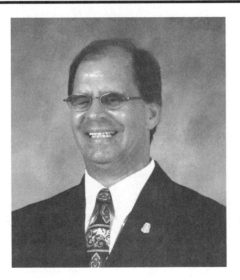

"The only lightless dark is the night of ignorance and insensibility. We differ, blind and seeing, one from another, not in our senses, but in the use we make of them, in the imagination and courage with which we seek wisdom beyond our senses."

—Helen Keller, *The World I Live In*

B obby Smith lay on the pavement in a pool of his own blood. He could feel it running down his face, wet and warm, but that was good. It meant he was still alive. He thought about his mother, who had died when he was ten years old, and his daughter, Kim, who was now ten.

I can't die on this pavement, he thought. *I can't do that to her*.

Bobby thought about the rabbit he had watched that morning while he was plowing a field. A hawk had stalked the rabbit relentlessly until, when there was no more field to plow, no hiding place left for the creature, the hawk had swooped down from the sky, its fierce claws capturing its prey. It was survival of the fittest, and Bobby knew as he lay there that he had to be strong to survive. As strong and determined as that hawk.

Bobby felt no pain. He couldn't see anything, but he could hear Jimmy Buffet's voice on his car radio singing "Cheeseburger in Paradise."

I like mine with lettuce and tomato

Heinz 57 and French fried potatoes

Bobby thought about the apostle Paul on the road to Damascus, on his way to kill the Christians. God had struck him down. Blinded him.

"Please, God, give me one more chance," Bobby prayed. "If You give me the chance You gave Paul, I'll be a better man, a better husband, a better father."

Bobby heard rapid gunfire, six shots, exploding around him.

And then he heard Deputy Don McDuffy screaming into the radio, "Get me an ambulance now. Trooper down. I repeat, trooper down."

B obby Smith grew up in Deville, Louisiana, a rural town outside of Alexandria. His father, Darwin Lavon Smith, was a World War II veteran who worked as a nurse at the nearby Veterans Administration (VA) hospital, and his mother, Alma Huffman Smith, was a homemaker. His parents were committed Christians, and theirs was a happy home, filled with the laughter of Bobby; his twin sister, Betty; and his two older brothers, Danny and Terry.

In 1952, the year Bobby was born, Alma was diagnosed with a little-known disease called "pemphigus"—an autoimmune disease that causes large blisters to form on the skin and mucous membranes. Hers was one of the first cases diagnosed in the United States, and several doctors from England came to Louisiana to study and treat her. Back then, there was no cure for this disease, and as Bobby got older, his mother's condition worsened.

By December 1962, it was apparent to everyone, including Alma, that she would not live much longer. "I am not going to die until I see my baby's birthday," she said to her husband as he sat by her bedside holding her hand. Alma was true to her word. She passed away on the twelfth of December—Bobby's tenth birthday.

"Losing her broke my heart," Bobby said. "After she died, relatives and people from our church helped Dad raise us. We lived in a rural community where everybody helped each other, but it was a difficult time."

A few years later, Darwin married Edith Honeycutt, the nursing director at the VA hospital where he worked. Before long, they had a son, Kevin. "Edith was a good mother to us, and we loved Kevin. He was never our half brother. He was our brother," Bobby said.

In sixth grade, Bobby met Jackie, the girl who would one day become his wife. "I played on the football team, and she was a majorette. I can still remember where I was sitting the first time I saw her," Bobby said. The two remained sweethearts throughout junior high and high school and married soon after they graduated.

Bobby had no aspirations to attend college, partly because an English teacher in high school once told him, "You're never going to college. You'll never pass." Bobby simply wasn't interested in school. He had maintained a 2.6 GPA, but that was only so he could play sports. He was more interested in being the class clown, in having fun. Two years later, D. K. Murphy, an electrical contractor and friend, convinced Bobby that he needed to have a degree if he wanted to become successful in life.

Bobby began his college career at Louisiana State University in Alexandria, majoring in special education, before moving to Northeast Louisiana University, now the University of Louisiana at Monroe. "I was still majoring in special education, but then I met some cops in one of my classes. I thought they were so cool. They'd tell us war stories, and one day, I asked if I could do a ride-along. They let me ride with them on a busy Friday night, which involved some car chases and bar fights. I knew I had to get me some of that, and I changed my major to criminal justice."

Bobby joined the Monroe Police Department in May 1975. "I probably took more drunks home than to jail," he said, laughing at the memory, but he gets more serious when he talks about domestic violence calls. "I couldn't handle those," he said. "I couldn't understand how any man could hit a woman. I'd just as soon hurt those guys when they hurt their wives."

Soon after he joined the force, on August 2, 1975, Bobby's daughter, Kim, was born. Bobby fell in love with his beautiful baby girl, but unfortunately, he and Jackie drifted apart. They divorced after five years of marriage but remained friends, and together, they raised Kim in a loving family environment.

Bobby enjoyed being a police officer, and the Monroe Police Department prepared him well for what had become his dream. He had worked traffic, burglaries, narcotics, and too-many-to-mention domestic violence calls, but he wanted to be a state trooper.

"I was turned down twice because of my knee, an old football injury," Bobby said. "Finally, I asked to sign a waiver that said if I hurt my knee in the academy, I would resign. I was so happy when I was finally accepted."

It's a common perception that the state police are the elite among police officers. Bobby disagrees because he has worked with many fine officers from city police departments and sheriff's departments, but there is a difference in the way state troopers are viewed, and Bobby wanted to be the best of the best. "In the academy, our instructor said, 'This badge is made of gold, and all others are made of silver,'" Bobby recalled. "I have to say that the training state troopers receive is top-notch."

In 1981, Bobby married Debra Lynn May, a former Miss Teen Louisiana, whom he had met through a trooper friend. He couldn't have been happier. He had a career he loved and a gorgeous wife. "I learned the hard way that sometimes beauty really is only skin deep," he would later say.

For the next few years, Bobby did what many state troopers do—worked traffic accidents and wrote tickets. He loved his job and made many lifelong friendships with other troopers.

On March 14, 1986, everything changed.

"I got up that morning and went to my farm to plow the field. We were preparing to plant our annual crops of soybean and cotton. When I finished, I went to the gym and trained for an upcoming powerlifting meet I was participating in," Bobby said. "Then I went home and took a shower. It was a day like any other."

He was scheduled to work the 2:00 p.m. to 2:00 a.m. shift and had just stepped into his car when he received a call from headquarters instructing him to call Lieutenant Don McDonald. He made the call and was assigned to work highway interdiction duty that day. Four state troopers and eight sheriff's deputies would meet in Winnsboro, Louisiana, and set up a drivers' license checkpoint. "We were to look for drugs, alcohol, and old warrants," Bobby explained.

That evening, red and blue lights flashing along Highway 15 warned impaired drivers they were about to be in trouble. Bobby didn't know that a man named Fred Anderson, Jr. had put five weapons on the passenger seat of his car before leaving his home that evening. A neighbor had asked him where he was going. "I'm going to kill a pig," Anderson replied. The neighbor thought he was going hog hunting.

At 11:35 p.m., Anderson sped through the checkpoint, his license plate painted blue, his inspection sticker removed. Bobby jumped in his car and gave chase. Deputy Don McDuffy followed close behind. Bobby pulled Anderson over.

He didn't wait for McDuffy to arrive. He got out of his car and walked toward Anderson's vehicle.

Anderson stepped out of his car, shooting. He fired once, wounding Bobby in his hand.

Bobby drew his weapon and returned fire, hitting Anderson in the left femoral artery.

Anderson fired again. This time, the bullet ripped into Bobby's face. He fell to the pavement.

McDuffy's car screeched to a halt. Anderson was walking toward Bobby. McDuffy jumped out and shot Anderson six times.

Police from everywhere converged on the scene.

"I never thought I'd get shot, not once in all my years as a police officer," Bobby said. "I was better than that. I was one of the best. And there I was, lying on that pavement. Later, I realized that my badge was gold, and Don McDuffy's was silver, but he saved my life that night."

Bobby knew before the ambulance reached the hospital that he couldn't see. He prayed it was a temporary thing, but the doctors soon informed him that he had lost his left eye and that his right eye had been severely damaged. When he had healed enough to leave the hospital, Bobby was hopeful that, with time, he would be able to see again. He was so grateful to be alive that the reality of his situation had not yet sunk in.

It would soon enough.

Even simple things became a challenge for the athletic trooper. He couldn't walk without running into things. He couldn't bend over without hitting his head. He couldn't eat or drink without spilling something. He couldn't pick out his clothes, match his socks. He couldn't read a book or watch television. He couldn't see his daughter when she came to visit. "Kim cried herself to sleep every night looking at my state trooper picture," Bobby said. "This was devastating for her."

Bobby stubbornly refused to give up hope. Every morning, he stumbled into his den and headed for a lamp that sat on an end table. If he put his face close to the bulb, he could feel the heat radiating from it and he knew it was on. When he stared at the bulb, he could see a glow in the distance. "It was like looking down a long, dark tunnel, and seeing a faint glow at the very end. That light gave me hope," he said. "I knew as long as I could see that glow, I would one day see again."

One morning, he got up and went to his lamp. The glow was gone. He turned the lamp on and off.

Nothing happened.

He hurried as fast as he could to the bathroom. Above the mirror, a row of Hollywood lights burned bright, but Bobby could not see a glow, no matter how hard he tried.

He slumped to the floor, realizing for the first time that he would live the rest of his life in pitch-black darkness.

"God, why did You take away my light, my one little glow?" he cried.

Suddenly, Bobby felt a presence in the room. Then he heard a voice. "You don't need that light. I am the light, and I will show you the way."

"What do You want me to do?" Bobby asked.

He received no answer.

Bobby sat on that bathroom floor and cried like a baby.

Realizing he was falling into a state of severe depression, Bobby decided he needed to return to work. He had always loved putting on that uniform. It made him feel proud. He knew he couldn't go back to his former position, but he thought there must be something he could do.

One morning, he got up early and donned his uniform. Edwin Edwards, the governor of Louisiana at that time, had called Bobby to express his sympathy. The governor had suggested that Bobby should go to work at the Louisiana State Police Training Academy. Edwards then called the colonel at the state police, whose name Bobby refuses to mention, and repeated the suggestion. Confident that he could be of some service, Bobby went to see the colonel, unaware that the colonel was livid because the governor had intervened.

"I told him I could be a benefit to the department," Bobby said. "He leaned back in his chair and said, 'Son, we no longer have a place for you. We don't need you anymore.'"

Bobby couldn't believe it. All of his trooper friends, his deputy friends, and his friends from the Monroe Police Department had been so supportive of him throughout his ordeal, but the colonel was telling him to go away. As he turned to walk out of the room, the darkness began to close in.

In August, three months after the shooting, Debra left him. "She didn't want to be married to a blind man with no future," Bobby said. "I was devastated. I had lost my sight, lost my career, and now my wife had left me."

Bobby couldn't take the pain. "The colonel said I had no worth. My wife left because my worth as a human being, as a husband, was gone. That night, I crawled across the floor on my knees and pulled out my service revolver."

He sat there holding it, feeling the cold metal, thinking about putting it to his head.

Then Bobby thought about his daughter, Kim.

That stopped him in his tracks.

Realizing he needed help, he put the gun down and called his friends—Mike Epps and Jackie Coleman from the Louisiana State Police, and Bobby Mann from the Monroe Police Department.

"For the first time, I said, 'I need help.' Before that, whenever anyone would ask, my pat response has always been, 'I'm fine.' I wasn't fine. They rushed right over. I told them, 'I'm dying inside. I'm afraid if I don't get some help, something bad is going to happen.'"

Bobby's police friends came through for him over and over for the next few years. When he called in the middle of the night, they showed up at his house, even when they had to work the next morning. Sometimes they brought him to their own homes to stay for a few days until they were confident he was okay.

With encouragement from his friends, Bobby went to see a therapist, but that didn't help. Then he heard Dr. Spencer J. Campbell, a former police officer and Army veteran, speak about trauma and loss. Bobby called and asked if the doctor would work with him.

"Under two conditions," Dr. Campbell said. "Never lie to me, and never lie to yourself."

Dr. Campbell worked with Bobby for six months and helped him tremendously. "He convinced me to go to a school for the blind," Bobby said.

By this time, Bobby was thirty-three years old and angry at the world. "I was like a hurt dog," he said. "I'm rebellious by nature, used to telling people what to do, not used to listening. I didn't like my instructor at all. I called her 'Nurse Ratchet.'"

Bobby soon got an idea and called his brother Kevin. He wanted to paint his cane regal blue, the color of his police uniform. Kevin painted the cane for him, and the next morning, Bobby proudly clicked along the corridor of the school. He was promptly sent to the director.

"The white cane is the international sign of blindness," the director informed him in a stern voice.

"Walking through Walmart knocking stuff off of shelves is a sign of blindness, too," Bobby retorted, and he refused to paint his cane white.

Not long after, Bobby had an altercation with another instructor who had insulted him. "I went after him," Bobby said. "Nurse Ratchet came to the door screaming my name. I sat quietly, so she couldn't tell where I was. She said I had to apologize. I wouldn't."

That was the end of blind school for Bobby, but he had learned enough there to be able to function in the world, to read braille, to walk through city streets safely, and to live alone without help, although his sister, Betty, stayed with him for a while.

In 1988, he met Janie Dupuy. Janie was a clinical dietitian and a licensed counselor. An intellectual, Janie was quiet, but strong, and she fell in love with the troubled man who couldn't see her. "Janie is so sweet and compassionate," Bobby said. "They tell me she's gorgeous, but I've never seen her. She feels pretty, and that's all that matters to a blind guy. I had to marry her, and it's the best thing I've ever done. I call her my angel girl because she became the wind beneath my wings."

In 1990, Janie gave birth to their son, Brad Elliott Smith. Bobby was ecstatic, and slowly but surely he began to feel like he had worth again. He had come a long way from crawling across the floor toward his gun.

Janie convinced Bobby that it was important for him to continue his education, and Bobby agreed, although the thought of navigating a college campus as a blind man scared him. Determined, though, he enrolled in Northeast Louisiana University, where he earned his master's degree in exercise physiology. Then he earned his Ph.D. in counseling/psychology. "I made one B in college," he said. "I missed that A by one-tenth of a point."

After graduation, Bobby found a new purpose quite by accident. He had filmed a training video, called "Incident on LA 15," for some of his police buddies. As a result of that video, he was asked to speak to a group of police officers. "I was very nervous," Bobby remembered. "They played the video, and then Louisiana State Trooper Aubrey Futrell introduced me. As soon as I got to the podium, I started to cry. I couldn't speak. I stood there in front of everyone with tears running down my face, and every time I would start to speak, I'd start crying again. Finally, I got through my story."

That was the beginning of a new career, as word about the blind state trooper spread. Police and other organizations around the country began to ask Bobby to speak at their events. By 1997, Bobby's life had turned around. He had a loving family and a purpose—teaching other police officers how to survive trauma. He also wrote a book, *Visions of Courage—The Bobby Smith Story*, about his life. "I typed it on a computer, then handed it off and said, 'Y'all fix it,'" he recalled, laughing at what he knows are his own limitations. "I wrote it for my own benefit. I didn't want to forget the details of what had happened to me."

Bobby didn't know it then, but his world had not yet finished spinning.

On September 29, 1997, Bobby got the call that every parent fears. His daughter, Kim, had been killed in a car accident in Monroe, Louisiana, where she attended college.

"She was only twenty-two years old," Bobby said. "I was devastated. She had been thrown out of the car upon impact. She was a beautiful person, and I couldn't imagine my life without her."

As usual, Janie pulled him through his darkest hours. She encouraged him to keep going, reminding him that he had a moral obligation to help others through his experiences. Together, Janie and Bobby worked through their grief, and then Bobby traveled the United States, speaking to schools, police organizations, and corporations in nearly every major city in the country. He also wrote another book, *The Will to Survive—A Mental and Emotional Guide for Law Enforcement Professionals and the People Who Love Them*, with Linda Severson. This book depicts the difficulties police face in their lives and their marriages as a result of their jobs. "It explains why we do the things we do," Bobby said.

In 2001, Bobby founded the FORTE Foundation (Foundation for Officers Recovering from Traumatic Events), a 501(c)(3) nonprofit corporation with the mission to "provide psychological services, educational workshops, and training conferences for the Louisiana law enforcement family." He recognizes that there are many dangers that police officers face other than bodily injury.

"Because of the job they do, this group is particularly vulnerable to unjustified guilt, resentment, trauma, and suicide," Bobby said. "We help police officers and their families through mental, emotional, physical, and spiritual healing."

For the next seven years, Bobby counseled other officers, never dreaming that he might one day proudly wear a blue uniform again. In 2008, Bobby was sitting next to Colonel Mike Edmonson at a luncheon where he was scheduled to speak. Mike, who had recently been promoted, reached over and grabbed Bobby's hand.

"You're coming back to the state police." Mike said.

"No, I'm not," Bobby said.

"Yes, you are."

"No, I'm not."

"Yes, you are."

"I was not welcome there," Bobby said.

"You are welcome," Mike said.

"I'm not wearing a uniform," Bobby said.

A few weeks later, Bobby stood in front of Mike, dressed in his Louisiana State Trooper uniform, as Mike pinned his gold badge on him. "I started crying when I got that uniform," Bobby said. "It was so emotional for me. I love these guys, and I love being a state trooper."

Coming full circle, Bobby went to work at the training academy as the director of the Troopers Assistance Program. It meant so much to him to be of value to the agency once again. Bobby was a happy man. Every morning, he got to wake up next to Janie and then go to work at the academy. His son, Brad, now a student at the University of Louisiana at Lafayette and a model for Hanes clothing, was doing well.

In 2009, Brad helped Bobby with his third book, *What's in Your Heart Comes Out Your Mouth*, written with Val Penouilh. This book focuses on the power of words and the power of forgiveness. "I'm most proud of this one because Brad helped me with it," Bobby said.

In November that year, he wrote his son a letter. "Merry Christmas," he wrote. "Smiles in my heart." In the letter, he included stories about when Brad had been born, stories from his childhood, stories from his teenage years. He told Brad how much he loved him and what it meant to him to be his father. Brad cried when he read that letter. He told Bobby it was the best Christmas present he had ever received.

Two months later, on February 22, 2010, at the age of twenty, Brad died of an accidental drug overdose.

Bobby's heart was broken again. There had been no warning, no clue that this would happen.

"That was so hard," Bobby said. "I'm a father. I kept asking myself, 'What did I do so wrong that my son would make a choice that would take his life? I don't know the answer to that. What I do know is that God is all-knowing. He knew when Brad would be born, and He knew when he would die. If you believe that, there's nothing you can do to change it. God doesn't make mistakes. Now I tell parents, 'Don't take your children for granted. You are not promised they will be here tomorrow. Treasure every moment you have with them.'"

It has now been thirty years since Bobby lay bleeding on that pavement the night he lost his sight, almost nineteen years since Kim died, six years since Brad died. Bobby still struggles with grief from time to time, but Janie is always there to hold him close. As he walks down the long, familiar corridor that leads to his office at the academy, he passes by a large shadow box on the wall filled with his accomplishments. He can't see them, but he knows they are there. And he knows why they are there—because God gave him another chance and because an angel loves him.

Bobby and Janie plan to move to Alexandria next year to open a FORTE Foundation facility to help not only police officers, but also firefighters and emergency medical services personnel from all over Louisiana.

Bobby has learned the hard way that being blind isn't the worst thing that can happen to a person. "Life's not fair. We have choices. We can get bitter or get better," Bobby said. "I don't like being blind, but I'm not dead. I don't like the fact that my children are gone. It kills me, but I can sit on the couch bellyaching, or I can use my knowledge and my own experiences to help other people recover from stress, grief, and trauma."

With strength, love, and concern for those who have suffered as he has, Dr. Bobby Smith shines the bright light of hope.

For more information, please visit www.thefortefoundation.com.

MAURICE "TERMITE" WATKINS

Boxer trades cocaine addiction for Olympic victory

"Now, whoever has courage and a strong and collected spirit in his breast, let him come forward, lace on the gloves and put up his hands."

—Virgil, *The Aeneid*

T ermite Watkins' eyes filled with tears as the crowd erupted, standing to applaud Iraqi boxer Najah Ali Salah as he made his debut at the 2004 Olympics in Athens, Greece. It had been almost two decades since Iraq had been represented at the Olympics, and the fight to return had been the toughest fight of Termite's life—and the most rewarding.

A former American boxer, Termite had always wanted to compete in the Olympics, but that had not been in the cards for him. Instead, he had gone another route, a route that had brought him here to this moment, to this fight.

With bombs exploding around them, Termite's challenge had been to train the Iraqi team in only fifty-seven days. Most competitors spent their whole lives training for the Olympics. Termite knew it would be a miracle if he succeeded. Despite numerous obstacles along the way, he had readied the team and persuaded the International Olympic Committee to agree to allow Iraq to participate.

And here they were, the applause getting louder and louder.

Termite swallowed his tears and gave his instructions. "Najah, keep him in the center of the ring. Outpoint him. Jab to the head. Jab to the body. Jab to the head. Right hand to the body. Don't throw any hooks, all straight punches."

Then he kissed him on each cheek. "I love you, son."

The bell rang.

B y the time he was six years old, Maurice Watkins, who had been nicknamed "Termite" at birth, was staying up late at night drinking beer and smoking cigarettes with his uncle. His father, Bill, was a gangster who owned a pest control company and dabbled in drugs and alcohol. Occasionally, when circumstances warranted, Bill would use his fists to make his point. In Termite's family, fighting was the normal outcome if someone looked at you the wrong way.

Termite's mother, Wanda, tried to steer her family in the right direction, and despite Bill's off-and-on approach to drugs and alcohol, he was not a bad father to his son. "When he wasn't drinking, he was a loving father," Termite said, "When he was drinking, we knew to stay out of his way."

Termite grew up alternating between going to church with his dad during the good times and steering clear of him during the bad times. Bill was tough, mean as a tiger when he was drunk, but Termite respected him and wanted to please him. When Bill said Termite should play baseball, the young boy tried his best, but he just couldn't catch a ball. Every time a baseball sped his way, it sailed on by because Termite was easily distracted by people in the stands, the birds flying overhead, anything but what was going on in the game.

Bill gave up on the idea of baseball, but he knew his son needed something to keep him out of trouble. He was determined that Termite would not end up like him. When Termite was ten, Bill insisted that he take up boxing. At sixty-five pounds fully dressed, Termite wasn't the best candidate for that sport either. However, after Termite lost his first fight, Bill realized his son had a winning spirit. No matter how many times he got punched, Termite stood there, refusing to fall to the mat.

Encouraged, Bill talked to Kenny Weldon, at that time an undefeated professional boxer. At first, Kenny balked at the idea of training a kid who didn't know how to box, but Bill was insistent. "He gets into four or five fights a week on the street. I want him to learn to fight the right way," he told Kenny. Finally, Kenny agreed to watch Termite fight. He observed Termite's street-fighting style and knew he had his work cut out for him, but he also saw the same thing Bill had seen. The boy had grit. He was stubborn. Kenny, who would later go on to train Evander Holyfield and Sergei Kobozev, agreed to take on the challenge. Termite soon found himself going through rigorous workouts and learning the fundamentals of the sport.

Under Kenny's tutelage, Termite began to win fight after fight, his fists meeting each opponent's face in a flurry of gloves, each fight boosting his confidence. His left jab, relentless in its assault, followed by an unexpected right hook, took out opponent after opponent over the next few years. Termite worked hard. He got up at 5:00 a.m. and ran around his neighborhood, went to school, worked out after school for several hours, did his homework, and went to bed.

"I quit fighting on the street and concentrated my efforts in the gym," Termite said. "Boxing kept me on the straight and narrow throughout my teenage years. My dad gave me all the support a kid could want. He got me the best trainers, took me to the best gyms, really spent a lot of time pushing me to be the best I could be."

And Termite had something to prove. After Kenny's boxing career became too demanding for him to continue as Termite's trainer, Termite began working with a new trainer, Albert "Potato Pie" Boulden, who was known as a master of the technical side of boxing. His no-nonsense approach forced his fighters to work hard to win his approval. By the time Termite qualified for the Texas Golden Gloves Championship in 1973, Potato Pie had made sure his protégé was ready. Termite won a hard-fought match and became the state champion. He went on to fight in the National Golden Gloves Championship and became the first sixteen-year-old in boxing history to win that title.

At sixteen, Termite also began attending church with his girlfriend. He had gone to church throughout his childhood when his father wasn't binging, but this time was different. He was determined that it was time to become one of the good guys. When the preacher asked, "Where would you go if you died?" Termite decided he wanted to go to heaven. He became a Christian that day and soon began spreading God's word to his friends at the gym.

His boxing career took off.

When he was seventeen, Termite turned pro. His goal was lofty. He wanted to become the world champion. His father became his manager, and Termite quickly earned a reputation as the boxer who never gave up. He could bob, weave, and punch his way to unexpected victories over more seasoned boxers. His record was 25-0 before he lost his first fight.

"My father managed my career," Termite said. "We got to spend a lot of time together."

At times, he toured on the USA Team with other boxers, such as Sugar Ray Leonard and Howard Davis. At one point, Termite was offered a fortune to place his career into the hands of a new manager, which would mean firing his father. "My dad said I should think about it, but I just couldn't do it," Termite said. "We had come too far together. We were too close, and I knew what he had done for me. He had gotten me to the top."

The "top" became a world championship fight held October 2, 1980. Termite was slated to fight Saoul Mamby in the junior welterweight division in a double main event. Termite didn't know it at the time, but this night would go down in history.

Also on the card were Muhammad Ali and Larry Holmes.

Termite had conditioned for this fight since he was a child. He wanted the championship with every fiber of his being and he fought hard—so hard that, by the end of fifteen rounds, both boxers were injured. Mamby, the reigning champ, won in a controversial decision.

Ali also lost that night. That would be his last fight.

In the space of a few hours, two of America's most promising boxers ended their careers.

For the next eighteen months, Termite tried to deal with the pain he felt over his fall from grace by partying at country and western clubs, dancing into the wee hours of the night. With a smile plastered on his face, he signed autographs and shared stories of his favorite fights. Inside, he felt like he had let everyone down.

Then he met Sharla, a young mother who captured his heart. Termite and Sharla married, and Termite became a father to Sharla's son, Jared. He returned to boxing and began winning again, but injuries eventually forced his retirement.

During his career, Termite earned a 58-5-2 record with forty-eight knockouts. At twenty-six, he was unsure what his future would hold. Fighting was all he had ever known. His face had graced the cover of *Sports Illustrated* and other prominent magazines; he had spoken to children in schools across the country; and he had earned a fortune, but he felt like a failure because he had lost the most important fight of his career.

He began hanging around with celebrities—football players, musicians, actors.

"I was very young when I retired from boxing, still a kid, really," he explained. "I thought I was hot stuff. Everyone wanted to be around me. I got caught up in it. Somewhere along the way, I started living my life for other people. I was always performing, even in my personal life. I felt like I had to prove myself over and over."

In his marriage, too, Termite felt like he had to prove that he was worthy of his status as a husband and father.

The pressure began building. One day, a friend invited him to a party where Termite was offered his first line of cocaine. He was in the wrong place at the right time in his life. He embraced the euphoria that accompanied his first taste of cocaine and spent the next five years chasing that initial high.

"I became a functional addict," he said. "I had opened a bail bond company, so I know all of the criminals and drug dealers. It was very easy for me to get whatever drugs I wanted. My life spiraled downward."

While his Christian values were still intact, suddenly Termite found himself living in a world beyond his control, a world marred by drugs and death. One night, he went out to get two ounces of pure cocaine. He had the coke in his hands when something told him to give it back and get out of the house. He gave the drugs back and had turned to leave when a man walked in and said, "What are you doing here? You need to leave."

Termite left.

He later learned that the two men who had given him the drugs had been murdered.

Another time, he went to a dealer's house to get some drugs, but nobody answered the door. Two weeks later, Termite learned that his drug dealer had been found dead, wrapped up in a piece of carpet in the garage of his home.

Termite knew that the life he was living was dangerous. His nose was bleeding all the time. He was spending all of his money on drugs. He was out of control, and everyone close to him knew it.

"Sharla gave me a reason to quit," he said. "One day, I called her, and she said, 'Don't come home.' I asked, 'What do you mean?' She said, 'You've got some decisions to make.' I knew she was serious. We had two children by then, and I didn't want to lose my family. I knew I had to change."

Termite went to see his pastor and best friend since childhood, Johnny Brady. "I was telling him what he wanted to hear," Termite said, "but I wasn't fooling him. He came unglued on me. We began praying, and I rededicated my life to serving God right then. That was thirty years ago."

Termite ended the unsavory friendships he had made and kicked his habit. It wasn't easy. Temptation was everywhere, and Termite didn't trust himself. Whenever he drove through the old neighborhoods, he made sure that he always had someone with him. He began speaking at schools and churches, hoping his experiences would keep others from traveling the same road. He knew by exposing his mistakes, he would be forced to live up to the advice he gave. It was insurance for him, in a way.

Through the course of his recovery, Termite realized that he had put his family through a lot. He had made a good sum of money in his career, but that was all gone now. He worked in his father's exterminating business, and he was surviving, but he wanted more for his family. They had paid a high price for his dreams, and Termite knew they deserved better from him. He took a job as a car salesman and soon realized he had a talent for sales. He worked hard over the next decade to give his family financial security, but cracks were beginning to surface in his marriage.

In 2003, Termite was given the opportunity to travel to Iraq to serve his country. He had been as disturbed as everyone by the events of September 11, 2001, and he jumped at the chance. He agreed to help rid U.S. military camps of bugs, snakes, and rodents. In the middle of the Iraq War, Coalition Leader Mike Gfoeller learned that Termite was a former professional boxer, and he challenged Termite not only to build an Iraqi boxing team, but also to get them to the Olympics. This would prove to be an almost insurmountable task, riddled with bombs, unfamiliar customs, and only a short time to perform this miracle, but Termite was up for the challenge.

Many months and many miles later, as he watched Najah Ali fight his first Olympic bout against Kwak Hyok Ju of North Korea, Termite couldn't have been prouder. Najah took the first round and then the second, the third, the fourth. Then the announcement came: "From the country of Iraq, Najah Ali."

In a small village in Baghdad, guns once used for war fired rapidly into the air in celebration of this monumental victory.

Termite bowed his head and thanked the Lord for giving him that moment, for giving the whole country of Iraq such a proud moment.

Najah lost his next bout, but it didn't matter. When asked by a reporter how he felt about the loss, Najah responded, "I'm free. My country is free. I just represented my country in the Olympics, and the world loves me. Did I lose?"

Termite's experience at the Olympics was bittersweet. "I wanted to go to the Olympics as a kid, but instead I went the professional route. The way I got there was through helping someone else. That's what life is all about."

Due to Termite's efforts, Iraq was represented in many sports at the Olympics that year. His experience in Iraq proved to be a turning point in his life.

Hailed as a "miracle worker," Termite returned home. In 2005, the Boxing Writers Association of America presented him with a Special Achievement Award to honor him for what he had accomplished in the midst of a war. Later that year, *Intersport* named Termite as its Arete Award winner. The Arete Award symbolizes glory, virtue, and excellence. Termite once again enjoyed celebrity status, but this time, he understood the ramifications of fame and knew better than to get carried away with it.

Unfortunately, Termite's time in Iraq had put a tremendous strain on his marriage, and he and Sharla eventually parted ways.

A few years later, Termite met Cindy, a divorced mother with four daughters.

Cindy had no idea that Termite had once been a famous boxer. He was simply the guy who exterminated her home. For the first time, Termite felt like he didn't have to be a celebrity. Cindy loved him for the person who she knew, an ordinary man who lived his life to serve the Lord. In 2011, Cindy and Termite were married.

"I want to court her and date her for the rest of my life," he said. "She's the sweetest person I've ever met. I no longer wonder if I'm loved because I'm a boxer. I know I'm loved just for me, and it's the best feeling in the world. Through Cindy and her incredible faith in God and me, I became the man I always wanted to be."

Five years ago, Termite founded Fighter Nation, a boxing ministry that trains athletes to box and also hosts weekly Bible classes for them. In 2012, Marlen Esparza, a boxer from Termite's gym, became the first woman boxer from America to compete in the Olympics. She took home the bronze medal.

Through helping others achieve their dreams, Termite has found a new way to become a champion. "Jesus Christ saved me from a certain death and gave me eternal life. It's my turn now to do what I can to help others," Termite said.

He continues to dedicate his life to God; his wife; his children, Shawnah, Jared, and Tessa; and his stepchildren, Courtney, Karis, Christiana, and Kaitlyn. He also enjoys spoiling his eleven grandchildren.

In November 2015, Termite's father, his mentor through boxing and through life, passed away. "That was rough," Termite said. "He quit drinking decades ago and began living his life for the Lord. He was an incredible man, who always wanted the best for me. There were times I could have done better, but he was always there supporting me every step of the way. I miss him terribly."

Of all his accomplishments, Termite is most thankful that he is in a position to help kids find redemption and a better life. Through the Termite Watkins Charitable Foundation, he helps gang members, bullies, and convicts change their lives, and through Fighter Nation, he helps athletes find God. He is also working with soldiers who have undergone amputations in an effort to create an Olympic boxing category for amputee veterans. "I'd love for this to be an Olympic sport. These veterans have given so much of themselves for our country, and we need to support them in any way we can," Termite said.

For more information, please visit www.termitewatkins.com or e-mail Termite at termitewatkins@yahoo.com.

DAVID BOTTNER

Entrepreneur on a mission for the homeless

"Sometimes I'd see my father, walking past my building on his way to another nowhere. I could have given him a key, offered a piece of my floor. A futon. A bed. But I never did. If I let him inside I would become him, the line between us would blur, my own slow-motion car wreck would speed up. The slogan on the side of a moving company truck read, 'Together we are going places'—modified by a vandal or a disgruntled employee to read, 'Together we are going down.' If I went to the drowning man, the drowning man would pull me under. I couldn't be his life raft."

—Nick Flynn, author

F rederick stared at his son, David. "You never want to talk about your grand-mother," he said, irritation ringing in his voice.

"I really don't," David responded. "It was a bad time for me."

Frederick rolled his eyes. "What are you talking about?" he said.

David took a deep breath and then blurted out, "She used to abuse me. She kicked me. She beat me, and she did other things. She was beating me one time when you walked in."

Frederick thought for a moment. "I don't remember that," he said.

David described the apartment where his grandmother had lived when he was a child.

Frederick listened intently, his eyes widening as the memories came flooding back. "Oh, my God," he said. "I didn't realize she was beating you." He sat down and then looked up at his son. "She used to beat me, too."

David knew exactly what he meant.

───

D avid Bottner was born in 1972 in Lancaster, Pennsylvania, the son of Barbara and Frederick Christensen. Barbara had married his father when she was seventeen, and although she was very young, she tried to be the best wife she knew how to be. When David was almost four years old, his parents divorced. With Frederick gone, Barbara had to raise her son alone. She didn't have enough money to pay a babysitter, so Frederick's mother, Ginny, became her only real option for childcare. She believed the woman loved her son.

For the next year, David's grandmother abused the little boy—she beat him, she kicked him. Beginning at the tender age of three years old, she touched him inappropriately when she bathed him. David didn't understand what was happening to him. He only knew that his grandmother was forcing him to do things he didn't want to do. Fearful she would beat him again, the little boy did his best to follow her instructions.

When David was four, Barbara met a new man, Roger Bottner. The two married and moved to Vermont, where Roger was studying to become a geologist at the University of Vermont. It was a fortunate move for David. He was relieved that he no longer had to go to his grandmother's house, and he subconsciously buried the memories of what she had forced him to do. When he was five, Roger adopted him and became David's "real" father. For a while, David's life was happy. Upon graduation, Roger got a job with Amoco in New Orleans, and the family moved again.

A few years later, David's family received the news that his grandmother, who had become a prostitute, had been killed—shot to death by a boyfriend, who then killed himself, but David would not learn this until much later.

When David was ten, his younger brother, Julian, was born, and everything began to change. He was used to being an only child, used to getting all of the attention. Suddenly, Julian became the focus of the family, and David felt left out, alone, abandoned again.

David reunited with his biological father when he was eleven. "Things got weird for me then," he said. "We had received an invitation to attend my uncle's wedding, and my father was going to be there. Frederick was into training horses, using cocaine, and collecting money for the mob, but my parents did not know the extent of his dealings at that time. The meeting was awkward, but arrangements were made for me to visit with him in Pennsylvania the summer I turned twelve."

David eagerly anticipated the visit with his biological father, convincing himself that perhaps Frederick would give him the attention he felt he was lacking at home. He waited impatiently for months, excited to get to know his father. When summer finally arrived, David flew to Pennsylvania to stay with his uncle and visit with his father, but the day Frederick was scheduled to pick him up, his aunt called to inform David that Frederick couldn't see him. "He's too busy," David's aunt said.

"I was so upset," David recalled. "I just shut down. It was like being abandoned all over again."

Roger was a good father to David, but Roger's job took up a lot of his time. Nothing upset him as much as not having enough money, and when the family got low on funds, David could often hear him yelling about it. Even when David was very young, Roger ingrained into him the importance of having money. Heeding the lesson, David began working at a sweet shop when he was twelve.

When the family moved to a new neighborhood, David soon made new friends—friends who introduced him to drugs. "I knew Roger drank and smoked a little weed, so I would steal some of his weed, go sit on the railroad tracks with my friends, and get high," David said. "Drugs took the edge off, made me feel better about my life. They temporarily made me feel loved and made it easier for me to connect with my friends."

Barely a teenager, David began drinking and hanging out in the French Quarter. He also began having sex at an early age.

When he was fourteen, his biological grandfather came to New Orleans to see Pope John Paul II, who was visiting the city. "That night, I was visiting with my grandfather when he tried to set me up with some prostitutes. This was normal behavior from that side of my family," David said. "Everything was very dysfunctional."

David soon began getting into fights and underachieving in school, doing just enough to get by. He enjoyed sports, though, and excelled in soccer, football, and baseball throughout junior high and high school.

When he graduated from Clifton L. Ganus High School, he invited Frederick to come to his graduation. "I wanted him to see me graduate," David said. "I wanted to show him that I was going to be a success. He took me out drinking that night to celebrate."

Frederick asked David to move to Houston to work with him at a car dealership. David agreed. "That summer, I did my first line of cocaine with my father," he said.

David returned to Louisiana and attended Louisiana State University for three semesters, then transferred to Southeastern Louisiana University for another semester before he realized that college wasn't for him. "By this time, I was either living in my car or sleeping on a friend's couch. Sometimes I would shack up with a random woman just to have a place to stay. I had no direction. I had holes in my shoes and not much in the way of clothes. My mom and dad had moved to Chicago, and Frederick had moved to Albuquerque, New Mexico. I was still using coke and partying as much as I could. I was all alone at twenty, trying to do life, searching for anything that would fill the huge hole I had in my heart."

David quit school and got a job at Lakeside Toyota in Metairie, a suburb of New Orleans. It was there that he began to come into his own. "I felt like I had a family again, and I discovered I was really good at selling cars. Money was my god, and I quickly became the number one salesperson," he said.

Eighteen months later, David was hired at Ray Brandt Dodge on the West Bank of New Orleans as a sales manager. He attracted girls by driving sporty demos and began partying more than ever. "I got my own apartment, bought a car, and thought I finally had what I was looking for," he remembered, but the emptiness that had always lived inside of David was still there.

At the age of twenty-two, David married Barbara, a woman sixteen years older than he was. "I needed to be loved so badly that I guess I was looking for a mom," he said. "That was a very tumultuous time. I was married, but that didn't curtail my extracurricular activities at all. I didn't love myself, so how could I love anyone else?"

When he was twenty-seven, David took a general sales manager position at Big Ford in LaPlace, Louisiana, and became even more successful. "Everything I touched in the car business turned to gold," he said. "Up until that point, I had managed my addiction by doing drugs only on weekends, but then I started getting into trouble."

David received three citations for driving under the influence (DUI), and although he had been able to buy his way out of them, he began to have trouble keeping a job. The DUIs made it more difficult for him to get a new job, but he was finally hired at Adrian Vega's Ford Lincoln in Slidell, across Lake Pontchartrain from New Orleans. He got fired when he got his fourth DUI.

"I was bad off," he said, "partying, using drugs, having affairs."

David decided to go on the road selling cars for a marketing company. "I went to dealerships around the country, teaching them how to host special events where they could sell a lot of cars in four or five days. The dealerships loved me, and I began making about $30,000 each week."

That stopped for a while when he was sentenced to six months of house arrest. David could not stand being stuck at home where he was unable to increase his wealth, so he made the decision to quit drinking and driving. "I was a moron," he said. "I didn't quit for any other reason than that I wanted to make money."

The week after he was released from house arrest, David went out, bought some ecstasy, hired a limo so he wouldn't have to drive, went to a casino, and made up for lost time. Soon, he opened his own marketing company, Level 10 Marketing, and, as he says, he went on a "crazy man" spree. "I was living the life—traveling to Cancun, Miami, San Diego for the Super Bowl, and getting women to join me. I was doing a lot of coke, but by now, it was making me paranoid, so I switched to ecstasy. It made me feel loved and gave me the ability to love everyone. I was spending, spending, spending."

By the time he was thirty, David was amassing a fortune, but his marriage was falling apart. Finally, he divorced Barbara because he couldn't bear to destroy her life along with his own. "I hit bottom then. I felt so bad about the way I had treated her that I gave her almost all the cash we had. I wanted to buy her forgiveness."

By 2003, David was spiraling more and more out of control. The drugs, the women, the money, none of it filled the void in his soul. One day, he was working a sale in California when his bookkeeper called to inform him that he was $75,000 in the hole. David couldn't believe where all of his money was going. He flew back to New Orleans to attend a Saints game and did what he always did when he couldn't handle the stress—partied as hard as he could.

When he got home, his girlfriend, Emily, was there waiting, excited to see him. Still upset by the news he had received earlier that day, David drunk-dialed his other girlfriend when Emily left the room. He was still on the phone when she returned.

"Who's that?" Emily said, her voice rising with her suspicions.

"Nobody," David said, hurrying into another room.

Emily chased him. "Who is she?"

"Come pick me up," David said into the phone.

Ignoring Emily, David ran into the bedroom to change clothes. Emily followed close behind, questioning, yelling, and in David's mind, nagging. He swatted at her with the jeans he had picked up from the bed, trying to get her to leave him alone. He did not think about the belt still attached to the jeans.

The buckle hit Emily on the top of her head. David watched in horror as blood seeped from Emily's wound.

His first thought was, *I'm going to jail.*

"I'm so sorry. I didn't mean to do that. Emily, are you okay?" he said.

Crying, Emily turned and ran from the room.

David couldn't believe what he had done. He couldn't believe his life had come to this. Yes, he had issues, but he was not the type of man that would ever hit a woman, even accidentally.

"The next morning, I looked in the mirror, and I didn't like what I saw. I couldn't believe I had done that. I got in my car and went for a drive."

As David drove across the Twin Span Bridge over Lake Pontchartrain, he thought about driving off. "I literally wanted to die," he said. "I really didn't know who I had become. I hated myself. I had everything the world says you should have—beautiful girls, cars, houses, and a big, fast boat, but I was so mean, so miserable. I was lost."

Just before he steered his car into the concrete side of the bridge, David thought about a friend, who had told him about a church in Slidell—Harvest Church. He thought about his mother, who had been saved not long before. He thought about all the times she had said she was praying for him. He decided that it was time to see if this God was real.

"I went home and told Emily how sorry I was, and I asked her to go to church with me. We went to that church, and while the pastor was preaching, it hit me how very sorry I was for everything I had done, for all the people I had hurt in my life. The pastor's words revealed the freedom that could be found through the love of Jesus Christ. For the first time, I heard in my heart that I could be forgiven. Emily and I went back every week after that, and I gave my life to the Lord. God became real to me, and I had never felt so free in my life. Two months later, Emily and I were baptized."

While David's love for the Lord became real, God and money shared equal time as the rulers of his life. One day, during a prayer session at church, David walked to the altar and asked his pastor, Ken, to bless his business. While the pastor was praying, David heard God speaking to him. "God told me to marry Emily," he said.

David couldn't believe what he was hearing. Through his experience with his first marriage, he knew he had a problem. He never wanted to put another woman through the things his first wife had suffered. "I was thinking, 'No way. I can't be faithful,' but by the end of that prayer, I knew I had to marry her," David said.

Emily and David were married seven days later. "From the moment we got married, my business exploded. God worked miracles," David said. "I opened a business called 'Rush Hour Events' in Chicago and another Level 10 Marketing in Tampa. My friend, Johnny Lonarda, ran the Tampa business, and my friends, Jim Davis and Robert Hovey, ran the Chicago business. I was making millions fast and furious."

As soon as David was saved, he quit drinking, gambling, using drugs, and having affairs with other women. "God changed me. The old David didn't exist anymore," he said.

David was aware, however, that something still wasn't right. One evening, when he was thirty-seven, he and his mother were praying together. "All of a sudden, I got really scared. It was dark, and I was shaking," David said.

"Ask the Lord to show you what you want to know," his mother said.

David asked God to give him understanding.

"Suddenly, I saw a clear image of my grandmother making me do things to her," David said. Slowly, over time, the images kept recurring—the bathtub, the beatings, the abuse.

"God was trying to help me understand my own perversions, why I became who I was. I had trouble believing such horrible things, but the memories became clearer and clearer." Soon after, David had an argument with Frederick and discovered his grandmother had also abused his father.

As David's faith became stronger and his understanding increased, the way he processed pain began to change. Through this emotional growth, David found the forgiveness necessary to mature as a person and as a servant of God. "I hurt for my grandmother, and I forgave her," he said.

Finally free of his past, David was able to truly love his wife and others because now he could love himself.

In 2007, he went on a mission to the Philippines. While there, God spoke to him and told him to open a Dream Center in New Orleans. Dream Center is a volunteer organization that addresses medical, physical, and spiritual needs of inner city families. David spoke briefly with executives at a Dream Center in California, but he decided instead to open a Mitsubishi dealership in Baton Rouge with the hope that it would one day fund the ministry. Since his conversion, David had focused on hiring recovered addicts, giving them a second chance, and feeling good about the fact that he was helping people. Seeing the change in their lives gave him a great sense of purpose.

"I still didn't get it. Money was, as it had always been, my primary focus."

In August 2008, the stock market took a dive. "I went reeling," David said. "I lost millions on the dealership and the marketing company, more on a pizza company and a credit repair company. I had too many irons in the fire, and I had taken my eyes off God. The IRS was after me for a ridiculous amount of money, the attorney general was after me for false advertising, my ex-wife was suing me for $800,000, and Mitsubishi Motors wanted $2.3 million that I owed for floor plans and cars. I owed about $13 million altogether."

By now, David had two children and more responsibility than ever. "I remember lying on my bathroom floor asking God what I had done to deserve this. I came to a place of complete surrender, the place where, in my heart, I said, 'If You want to take it all, I guess it was all a gift anyway. I give up.' He said, 'Good, I never wanted you to do all this. I just wanted a relationship with you.'"

David awoke the next morning feeling at peace for the first time in a long while. Somehow he knew that everything would be okay. He gave Level 10 Marketing to a recovered addict he had once helped. He gave Mitsubishi its cars back and walked away from the dealership. The attorney general settled for $500. The court determined that David had more than fairly compensated his ex-wife, and he was not required to pay her anything further. God took care of every battle David faced, one by one.

For the first time since he was twelve, David stopped working. Instead, he spent his time studying the Bible and getting to know God as a loving Father.

Soon after he quit working, David attended an Association of Related Churches Conference and spoke with the executive director of Dream Center. "He didn't remember me from 2007," David said. "He asked which church I pastored. I told him I was a businessman, and he completely lost interest. He looked right over my head. I thought, 'Wow, I'm a nobody.' It was a novel experience. Nobody cared who I was. I walked out thinking, 'I'm okay with that.'"

David sold his house on the water, his Mercedes, his $30,000 Rolex. He still had money, but it didn't have him. He decided to open a carwash and lawn care service with the idea that he would give jobs to drug addicts and homeless people. The catch was that they would have to agree to attend a Christian program. His goal was to give them a place to live, but he didn't quite know how to achieve that. A friend, Troy Duhon, suggested that he speak with a woman who worked in the New Orleans mayor's office and ask her if the city could donate some land for the project. The woman recommended that David speak with the people who ran the New Orleans Mission.

David called them, but it didn't work out.

Two months later, David learned that the mission was in danger of shutting down. He met with the board of directors and told them he would run it for free. They insisted on paying him, so David agreed to a salary of one dollar per year.

When David began running the New Orleans Mission, which was established in 1989 on Oretha Castle Haley Boulevard, it served approximately one hundred guests each night. Like too many large cities across the country, New Orleans has a massive population of homeless people, which grew to unbelievable numbers in 2005 after Hurricane Katrina. Over the course of many years, the shelter deteriorated to the point that it was unsanitary. Rats and insects scurried across the floors, and mold caused by a leaky roof stained the walls. Some of the homeless in New Orleans refused to go there, preferring instead to sleep under the interstate or in back alleys. David was determined to change that.

"The first thing God told me was, 'David, you focus on loving the people, and I will take care of the building,'" David said. Before long, donations began pouring in, and things at the mission began to improve. In 2014, David announced a $6 million renovation.

Today, the New Orleans Mission can house two hundred fifty-two people on regular nights and up to four hundred on nights when the weather is freezing. As part of the renovation, David is adding a day room with twenty-four-hour access. Instead of being forced out at a certain time, guests will be welcome to watch television, exercise in the weight room, use computers to search for jobs, or use the restrooms.

Most importantly, David instituted programs to help the homeless—many of whom are veterans, drug addicts, or victims of mental illness—to recover and to become followers of Christ. Through the discipleship program, residents learn to move from homelessness and helplessness to a life of honor and service to others. These men and women, who once lived hopeless lives, are now filled with hope about the plans God has for them. Through the ex-offender re-entry program, David and the staff work with former prisoners upon their release. They are taught life skills and job competencies, and they are required to participate in the discipleship program for one year. The mission also provides therapeutic counseling for substance abusers.

"Our goal is to heal the heart, mind, and body, as well as to provide vocational education so these men and women can turn their lives around," David said.

To that end, the mission also encourages creativity, and many of its residents participate in Mission Media, run by Steven Scaffidi, which teaches media skills, such as video production. In 2016, Mission Media Productions teamed up with BIC Media Solutions and took on the *Rock Bottom and Back* project. Participants in Mission Media interviewed and filmed several people featured in this book for a pilot episode to be shopped to television networks as a possible series. This partnership helped participants gain real-world experience in the field of video production.

Through the New Orleans Mission, the homeless can also pursue artistic and musical endeavors. "We want to be vocationally creative," David said. "It's easy to do construction or carwashes. We started culinary and media programs to encourage our people to stretch beyond the limits of their imaginations."

Recently, the New Orleans Mission acquired the K Bar B Youth Ranch in Slidell, which had closed in 2012. This fifty-eight-acre property, renamed Giving Hope Retreat, features several dormitories, a swimming pool, and a pond, and now serves as a home for those enrolled in the discipleship program at the mission. Here, residents receive counseling and workforce training, as well as spiritual training. This retreat takes people out of the urban shelter environment where they must sleep next to strangers and places them in a rural area where peace and comfort can be found. Currently, seventy-two men are living at the facility, learning the skills they need to live their lives successfully while being of service to others. By the end of 2016, there will be one hundred beds available for women.

Taking on the mission was a challenge, but David thrives on challenge, and now his whole life is focused not on money, but on rebuilding lives through God. He is doing the work of the Lord and enjoying every minute of it.

Emily and David now have three children: Mia, eleven; David, ten; and Ayla Grace, three. David is happier than he has ever been. The demons that once haunted him are gone. He understands that the things he experienced and his reaction to them were the building blocks that now enable him to help others with love, kindness, and understanding.

"The New Orleans Mission has evolved into the largest faith-based, full-service mission in the Gulf South. We serve approximately two thousand five hundred people every year—ten thousand so far, by the grace of God," David said. "I don't see homeless people and drug addicts in front of me. I see their pain. I once lived that pain. If they can get healing from that pain, they can be helped. Through Christ and the many caring folks who support our mission, we offer shelter, faith, and a better future to those who have lost all hope."

For more information, please visit www.neworleansmission.org.

TONJA MYLES

From the crack house to the White House

"I'd still thought that everything I thought about that night—the shame, the fear—would fade in time. But that hadn't happened. Instead, the things that I remembered, these little details, seemed to grow stronger, to the point where I could feel their weight in my chest. Nothing, however, stuck with me more than the memory of stepping into that dark room and what I found there, and how the light then took that nightmare and made it real."

—Sarah Dessen, *Just Listen*

Tonja Myles stared at the writing on the bathroom wall—"Tonja is a slut," he had written, among other vile things. Stunned, she read the words again. Tears made their way slowly down her cheeks as the realization set in.

He doesn't like me. He thinks I'm a slut. He told everyone. I thought he liked me.

Tonja really liked him, and she hated most boys with a passion that ran deep into her childhood.

She stood there for a moment, staring at the wall, memorizing the words. *I can't do this anymore*, she thought. *It's too hard.* Taking a deep breath, she wiped her tears away and walked out of the bathroom.

Later that afternoon, Tonja sat in her bedroom, staring at the bottle of pills she had retrieved from the stash in her dresser.

He said he liked me. I hate him. I hate all of them.

Tonja opened the bottle, checking to see if she had enough. It was almost full. Relieved, she reached for the glass of water she had placed on the nightstand.

Closing her eyes, she swallowed a pill.

And then another and another until the bottle was empty.

"MaDear," Tonja Myles cried, running into her grandmother's house. "I get to sing in the choir at church. They're gonna let me sing." The young girl twirled around, her beautiful white dress spinning, her ponytails bouncing up and down.

"Of course they're going to let you sing," MaDear said, smiling. Tonja was only seven, but everyone in the family knew she had a God-given talent. "I'll be sitting in the front row, watching. You'll sing just like an angel. I just know it."

"I've got to get home. I have to practice," Tonja said, kissing her beloved grandmother on the cheek.

"You go on, now," MaDear said, hugging her granddaughter. "I love you, baby."

"I love you, too," Tonja said. "This much," and she stretched her arms wide.

Tonja hurried home, anxious to stand in front of the long mirror in her room, hymnal in hand, practicing the songs that always made her happy.

When she got there, she noticed her father's vehicle wasn't in the driveway, but that wasn't unusual. Wilbert Richard served in the Navy and sometimes worked long hours to support his wife, Hattie, and his three children—Kevin, Tonja, and Sanja. Everyone called Wilbert "the drill sergeant," but he didn't mind. He liked being the boss. And while he could be somewhat stern at times, Wilbert was a fair man, determined to raise his family right.

When Wilbert wasn't home, Hattie and MaDear oversaw things, steering the children in the way of the Lord. The family attended church on Sundays, said their prayers, and minded their manners. "My grandmother and mom raised us to be very tight-knit, to have each other's backs," Tonja said.

Tonja grew up in Baton Rouge, Louisiana. Her family wasn't poor by any means, but not quite middle class, either. If they were lacking something, Tonja didn't notice. She was a happy child, full of life and love. From the day she was born, Tonja's lyrical voice uplifted her family. She sang in her bedroom when she was playing with her toys. She sang in the kitchen when she was helping with chores. She sang in the shower. No one minded, though. Her joy was contagious.

Everything changed when Tonja was seven. "I was molested by one of my brother's older friends," she said. At first, the young girl didn't understand exactly what had happened, but she felt ashamed nonetheless. She understood enough to know that it was bad. She also knew better than to say anything to anyone. She had been warned.

Over the next two years, the rapes continued, and Tonja retreated more and more into a shell, hiding what was happening to her from everyone. The happy little girl disappeared, and in her place, an actress emerged. She still sang in the choir, but the joy was gone. "I can still remember his scent, the dark space where it happened," Tonja said. "That doesn't ever go away. About eight years ago, I saw a picture of myself as a child in a beautiful white dress, and I remembered that girl with the bright eyes and ponytails. I cried, and I thought, 'Oh, my God. She died, and no one grieved for her. I died at seven years old.'"

By the age of ten, as happens with many victims of molestation, Tonja had become promiscuous. She began having sex with boys in her neighborhood and at school. And then she got into fights. Hattie was called to visit with the principal on numerous occasions after Tonja had been in a physical altercation with another student. "My parents noticed the change in my behavior," Tonja said. "My dad was very hard on me, but my mom had started drinking by that time, and she had her own issues to worry about."

The only thing Tonja really cared about was singing. When she was invited to join the Baton Rouge Community Chorus, founded by Dr. Valerian Smith, she excitedly told MaDear, who proudly attended her granddaughter's recitals. "I remember singing a song Dr. Smith wrote," Tonja said, reciting part of the lyric. "'I am just a child, I know. Everything I am will grow. Things that hurt when I was small grow much bigger when I am tall.' That turned out to be such a prophecy."

By the time she was a teenager, Tonja had severe anger and self-esteem issues. She began to lash out through sex. "Things that once disgusted me, I began to like," she said. "I started having sex with any boy I could get."

At sixteen, Tonja began smoking weed and soon graduated to pills and cocaine. "Before I knew it, I was a crackhead. When I first smoked crack, it felt like I was invincible, like I was in a fantasyland where there was no more pain. That feeling wasn't real, but when you're on crack, you're always trying to get that first high back. That's what makes it so dangerous."

Tonja tried to hide her lifestyle from her parents, but they could see that their daughter was sinking fast. They didn't realize how fast, and they had no clue what to do.

Then Tonja read that writing on the bathroom wall at her high school, and she went home and ate a bottle of pills. Her mother found her in her room, unconscious, covered in vomit. Hattie rushed her daughter to the hospital, where doctors pumped Tonja's stomach in an effort to save her life. MaDear sat by her beside, her hands folded, praying. God heard her prayers, and Tonja survived the first of what would be several attempts to kill herself.

Tonja emerged from the hospital even more bitter and angry, her self-esteem in shreds. Soon she began having sex with wealthy married men for money. "I thought, I'm giving it away, and not getting anything in return, so why not get paid for it?"

she said. "In a twisted way, I was making men pay for what had been done to me. I had so much anger in me, and sex made me feel powerful, like I was in control. The reality was that I was out of control."

Having a normal relationship with a man was impossible—Tonja was much too traumatized for that—and although she went on real dates sometimes, her reputation always preceded her. "I went on a date with a guy one time because I thought he was a decent guy, and I really wanted a decent guy to love me. I thought he was different. While we were at his apartment, he wanted to have sex. I said no. That's when things turned ugly. He beat me and raped me until I passed out," Tonja said.

When she regained consciousness, Tonja hurriedly put on her torn clothes and ran out of the apartment. She didn't report the rape. She couldn't. Who would have believed her? She simply buried it along with the rest and continued to seek solace in drugs—using them and now selling them.

Unlike some who travel this road, Tonja remained committed to her education, mostly because the "drill sergeant" was insistent upon that. After she graduated from high school, she enrolled at Southern University in Baton Rouge, where she majored in criminal justice. It didn't take long for her reputation to follow her, and she soon met another young man she liked. "I really thought he liked me. I thought we could have a normal relationship," she said. But one night while they were in bed, Tonja saw the closet door in the bedroom move. "He had friends in the closet watching me," she said, a slight pink staining her smooth caramel cheeks at the memory. "I began hitting him. 'How could you do this to me?' I cried. He thought it was okay because of my reputation."

Each time Tonja was injured, her wounds fueled her rage and her despair. When she was nineteen, she tried to kill herself again. This time, she reached out for help and spent thirty days in a mental health facility. However, when she was released, she ran right back to drugs and prostitution.

Her addiction to crack soon progressed to the point that Tonja didn't recognize herself. After she stole money from her parents to buy drugs, her father kicked her out. As she was leaving, Tonja yelled, "I'll fix y'all," and she promptly joined the military. Unfortunately, that was like putting a kid in a candy store. There were men everywhere. That only fed Tonja's sexual addiction. True to form, she began sleeping with anyone who would have her.

"I was brutally raped again," Tonja said, "but this time, I liked it. To be very honest, that's when I knew I was in trouble. It hit me then that I had no standards left. I stole from my parents, I slept with anybody who would pay me, and when I managed to say no, I enjoyed being forced to have sex. I thought, 'There's nothing left to me. I have become a monster.'"

Tonja hit rock bottom.

She went to a local park, determined to slit her wrists, but she discovered she couldn't do it. Instead, she ran to the woman who had always been there for her. She ran to MaDear's house. "I just fell into her arms," Tonja said. "She held me and told me that God had a plan for me. 'He will forgive you,' she said."

Tonja promised God that if He helped her, she would do everything she could to help others who were hooked on drugs. "The old Tonja died that day," she said.

Determined, Tonja quit using crack cold turkey. "I beat my drug addiction through faith and through the second chance my family gave me," she said. "I haven't looked back since. But the sex addiction was much worse than my addiction to drugs. I had never dealt with the trauma of being molested."

Tonja knew she had to change everything about herself if she was going to be able to fulfill her promise to God. She began attending church and reading the Bible, really listening to what the gospel was saying to her. She began to change the way she dressed, the way she talked, the way she walked. "I had to rehabilitate myself," she said. "Everybody had always told me I had something special, that I had gifts, but I had never listened. Everything, the people, places, and things in my life, had to change."

Tonja quit wearing makeup and deliberately gained weight. She tried to hide anything that would make a man want her. "I ran into an old friend one time, and she said I looked like a Jehovah's Witness. I said, 'Thank you.' That's what I was trying to do. I wasn't yet confident that I could turn my life around completely, and that was my way of warding off possible threats to my recovery."

Faith and family gave her the momentum; the military gave her the structure she needed to succeed. "I loved being a soldier," Tonja said, "and it was in the military that I first began to excel, to believe that I was capable of achieving success in my life." Tonja served nine years in the Louisiana National Guard as a military police officer, where she served her country with pride and dignity.

But she still wasn't satisfied. Tonja had made a promise to God, and she intended to keep it. About a year into her recovery, she realized that the non-denominational church she attended was not doing anything to help people with addictions. She wanted to start a ministry, but she wasn't sure how to go about it. Then she met Darren Myles, a man who lived his life to help others.

"He had never done drugs in his life, yet he had a passion for working with people in prisons, drug addicts, and those who were homeless," Tonja said. She admired the work he did and wanted to become involved. She and Darren became good friends and began ministering together. Wherever he preached, Tonja sang.

In 1993, Darren asked Tonja to marry him. She laughed at him. They were from two different worlds. He was from Mayberry, and Tonja's experience had been the polar opposite. A year later, Tonja changed her mind. "He knew about my past. In Darren, I finally found a good man, a decent man."

It wasn't easy. For seven years, Tonja had to be tested for the AIDS virus. She lived in fear that each year would be the year her past caught up to her. She and Darren had to go through intense counseling. "I still had that anger inside me, and fear. I told him, 'You are going to be in the mall one day, and someone will come up to you and say they slept with me. How are you going to handle that?'"

Darren saw through all of that. He saw her pain. He saw her strength. He saw the little girl who had sung in the choir. And he loved her, not despite who she had once been, but because of the beauty he saw inside of her. Together, they began a ministry called "Set Free Indeed" and began sharing their message of hope on street corners, in prisons, at nursing homes, anywhere they saw a need. The ministry was designed to reach people with any kind of physical or emotional problem—alcohol, depression, anger, drugs, gambling, pornography—and help them through recovery. Set Free Indeed, which started with ten people in a friend's house and eventually moved to MaDear's house, grew so large that Tonja and Darren began to hold meetings on Friday nights at local churches. Because Tonja could relate to the problems addicts faced and because Darren was so empathetic to their spiritual and physical needs, the ministry became more and more successful.

It was so successful that, in 2003, it garnered the attention of Jim Towey, then-director of the White House Office of Faith-Based and Community Initiatives. Jim asked Tonja if she had a problem sharing with America the life she had led and the success she had achieved. Tonja, in shock that someone from the White House had called her, said, "I'm pretty open about everything I've been through."

Towey asked if she had done anything that would bring shame to the White House.

Tonja thought for a moment—so much of her life had caused her shame, but she had not embezzled money or killed anyone. She said, "No."

Two days later, Jim called back and asked Tonja to be a guest of President

George W. Bush and First Lady Laura Bush at the State of the Union Address. Stunned, but elated, Tonja agreed to go to Washington, D.C., thinking she would be in a big room with a lot of other people watching the president speak.

She and Darren hopped on a plane. Hours later, they were in a motorcade heading for Capitol Hill. "I couldn't believe it when they led me to the first lady's box. They seated me beside her. She said, 'I'm so glad you're here, Tonja.'"

A few minutes later, Tonja listened as the president talked about the initiatives that were taking place in Baton Rouge through Set Free Indeed. Tonja, sitting next to Laura Bush, thought she would faint when everyone applauded, then turned to look at her.

After the address, Tonja and Darren attended a reception, where they met the president. "Tonja, we're so proud of you. I hope you liked what we said about you guys and the great work you're doing," President Bush said, after he hugged Tonja.

Nervous and excited, Tonja replied, "Thanks for the shout-out, Mr. President."

"Later, I wondered if he even knew what a shout-out was," Tonja said, smiling. "I was so nervous it just popped out."

Tonja was eventually invited back to the White House to participate in a Bible study fellowship. "That was such an amazing thing," she said. "I went from the crack house to the White House. It's unbelievable. There was a time when something like that would have seemed impossible to me."

Soon after, Tonja and Darren opened the Free Indeed Treatment Center, the first faith-based, licensed treatment center in Louisiana, in an effort to address the physical, mental, and emotional needs of addicts. However, Tonja did not like working in an administrative role. She preferred to be more hands-on, face-to-face with those she was trying to help.

Six years later, the couple sold the center and went back into the trenches where they felt they could do the most good. "We work with youth and adults. Addiction does not discriminate," Tonja said. "It affects people from the curbside to the country club."

Today, Tonja is a certified peer recovery specialist, a consultant, and an inspirational speaker. She works in three Louisiana prisons with inmates who have substance abuse and mental health issues. She teaches a class for female prisoners—"Women in Recovery"—in which she addresses anger management, job skills, good choices, and building healthy relationships. Tonja also speaks at schools, where she teaches children the danger of drugs, including deadly new synthetic drugs, and the power of choices. "Choose not to use" is the message the former addict preaches at rallies and school assemblies. "You don't have to get high to have a good time."

Tonja also hosts a weekly radio talk show on Cumulus Media—*The Tailgate: Real Talk, Real Results*—during which she discusses community and national issues. She works with Louisiana politicians and community leaders to bring about changes in policy and to raise awareness about substance abuse and mental health issues.

Sex trafficking is another major concern for Tonja. She counsels many young girls under the age of eighteen, helping them to regain their strength, self-worth, and value. "Abuse of young girls is becoming a rite of passage," Tonja said. "It's tragic. Molestation had become the norm, the same story told over and over by young girls who have been robbed of what could have been a happy, healthy life."

Because of the dedication and tireless energy Tonja brings to helping addicts through recovery, she earned the prestigious Substance Abuse Innovation Award from Johns Hopkins University. "I'm just happy I get to wake up every morning and do this," she said. "Every day, I wake up on a mission to help save someone's life. Everything I do is about community and empowering people."

It was only recently, though, while on a quest for truth, that Tonja finally addressed the trauma that had caused her to spiral downward. "That was so hard, facing that scared little girl in that dark room. I realized I am still suffering from the damage that was done to me at such a young age, but I power through it. Each time I help another addict find God, the pain moves a little farther away. I'm not over it. I will never be over it, but it doesn't control me anymore."

Darren and Tonja have now been married twenty-two years. Tonja still suffers from depression and post-traumatic stress disorder, but she forges ahead, trying not to dwell in the past.

"I thought I would be dead at the age of twenty-one, but I had a lot of people pulling for me," she said. "MaDear was the love of my life. She prayed me through a lot of really bad stuff. I would probably be dead if it weren't for her. And my father, he knew he had a warrior on his hands. He was so hard on me, but he always said I was special. I didn't understand him at the time, but I'm so grateful for him now. When I was little, my dream wasn't to grow up to be a crackhead. I'm glad I made it out. So many don't. If I can do it, anyone can."

For more information on how to get hope, help, and healing, please call (225) 288-1044.

JERRY STRICKLAND

Breaking the cycle of addiction

"Drinking gave me a rush of confidence, and for a boy hounded by feelings of inadequacy, the buzz was a welcome relief. What was impossible to realize at the time was that I was shooting myself in the head in some strange time warp where the bullet takes many years to finally reach its target."

—Brennan Manning, *All Is Grace: A Ragamuffin Memoir*

The full moon hung low over the snow-covered mountains, its light casting an ethereal glow on the twin peaks. Jerry squinted to get a better view and saw five pine trees, each taller than the next, jutting from the sides of the mountains. Two massive horses, both reared up with hooves pawing at the air and teeth bared, fought a battle for dominion. One was solid ebony, the color of darkest night. The other could have been its twin, except for a streak of white that weaved across its shoulder and down its immense frame.

Jerry watched intently, eager to see which horse would emerge the victor.

Then he was startled from his dream.

Disappointed that he would never know, Jerry got out of bed and began his day, the dream staying with him. He wondered what it meant because he rarely dreamed. Most nights, he fell into bed and slept the deep sleep experienced by many alcoholics.

He had no idea that this dream would change his life.

Jerry Strickland grew up in Blytheville, a small town in Arkansas, the son of Joe and Gladys Strickland. Like many families during the era following the Great Depression, they survived as well as they could in a rented home equipped with an outhouse. Jerry; his two brothers, Gene and Jimmy; and his sister, Sarah, shared bedrooms and took turns taking baths in the No. 2 galvanized washtub. Throughout Jerry's childhood, extended family members beset by circumstances beyond their control moved in and out. The door was always open at the Strickland home, and although food and space were sometimes limited, the family lived like almost everyone did back then. They stretched their dollars as far as they would go.

At times, life was good. Joe was a talented butcher, and there was always a need for a man who could carve every last morsel from a fresh pig. Other times, when Joe went on a bender, life for the family became more difficult. Joe didn't drink every day, or even every week, but sometimes he picked up the bottle, and he didn't put it down until he was good and ready. During those times, he couldn't be trusted with the sharp knives that were the tools of his trade, so the family had to make do any way they could. Once in a while, Joe would take up with another woman, then sober up and come back home, begging Gladys for forgiveness.

One time, when Joe was off drinking, Gladys, Jerry, and Sarah walked to the Liberty Grocery Store, where Joe worked, to buy groceries. They walked down each aisle, carefully selecting the items the family needed for the week, then headed to the checkout. During that era, it was standard practice to buy groceries on credit. As they waited for their groceries to be tallied, Mr. Henry, the owner of the store and Joe's boss, informed them that they would not be extended any more credit and could not take their groceries home. Even at the age of seven, Jerry understood what that meant, and he felt humiliated.

"I have never forgotten that," Jerry writes in his memoir, *Turnarounds—A Life of Inspiring Change*. "This was one of the most memorable moments of my life."

Jerry determined then and there that he would always have money, that his bills would always be paid. As a young boy, he began working a paper route, selling Coke bottles, candy, Christmas cards, and seeds, anything to earn the pennies necessary to save himself from being poor.

Although Jerry hated Joe's binge drinking, when he turned fourteen, Jerry experienced his first taste of whiskey and soon began drinking regularly. "It was a way for me to escape," he said. "Whiskey gave me courage, the confidence to ask girls to dance at high school dances. It changed me into someone I thought I wanted to be."

Eventually, Joe opened his own store. Jerry observed the process with avid interest, helping his father saw the lumber for shelves and stocking the canned goods that lined the shelves. He polished apples to a high shine and carried groceries to their customers' cars. Jerry learned about entrepreneurship from his father, and he soon began buying then selling half-pints of whiskey to his classmates, quickly doubling his money.

Although his parents had only an eighth-grade education, Jerry, after earning a two-hundred-dollar scholarship to Arkansas State University, decided to go to college. He obtained employment at a nearby hospital, hoping that between the hospital and his education he would develop the skills necessary to become a family doctor. This was a pipe dream. Jerry did not have the grades or money necessary to enter medical school. When he realized this, Jerry changed his focus to chemical engineering.

While in college, at twenty years old, Jerry married his high school sweetheart, Jimmie Lee Moore. They had grown up together, and marriage seemed to be the next logical step. It was also economically feasible, as they could get cheaper housing at the university if they were married. Soon after, the couple moved to Fayetteville to attend the University of Arkansas, where Jerry felt he would have better opportunities. There, he dedicated himself to his education. Jimmie Lee's family helped with the rent, and Jerry's family provided their groceries.

In January 1958, their first child, Jerry Strickland II (nicknamed Chip), was born. Finances became even tighter for the family, but in 1959, Jerry graduated, armed with a degree in chemical engineering and determined to become a success. The way to success, he thought, was to work in the oil fields. For years, he worked job after job—at companies such as Halliburton and BS&B. He made decent wages and was transferred to Texas and then to California, but he was nowhere near the success he envisioned.

Before long, Jerry and Jimmie Lee decided to have more children, but a doctor informed them that this would not be possible, so they adopted a daughter, Patia. Jimmie Lee's father, wanting his daughter closer to home, offered Jerry a partial partnership at his retail company, and Jerry and his family moved back to Blytheville. Although Jerry soon learned that the partnership was nowhere near equal, he found he enjoyed marketing and wheeling and dealing. It wasn't long, however, before he became dissatisfied with the arrangement with his father-in-law and decided to return to industry.

He worked several jobs, eventually landing in New York and then Boston. He also developed some bad habits. "I would usually go to lunch about 11:30 a.m. and have a couple of glasses of Scotch, then I would drive to an ad agent's office and have a drink or two. Drinking became a normal part of my daily routine. When I got home, I'd have a glass or two of chardonnay. At home, I had to be more careful because Jimmie Lee was always counting," Jerry said.

Jerry had no idea he had become an alcoholic. "Alcohol did not affect my work. Back then I thought it facilitated my work. I felt more creative, more verbal.

I could present my vision well. With a little alcohol under my belt, I could sell Popsicles to an Eskimo." Without alcohol, Jerry felt underappreciated, not respected for his capabilities.

With each new job, Jerry felt he was moving closer and closer to the fulfillment of his destiny, but the pressure to earn higher wages increased as his family expanded. He and Jimmie Lee had two more children, despite what the doctor had told them, and Jerry was determined that his children would never experience the humiliation that he had suffered as a child.

Throughout the seventies, Jerry made a lot of money for the companies that employed him. Soon he began to realize that he was spinning his wheels helping other people get rich while his income climbed at a slower pace. By 1976, he was earning $40,000 per year—a sizeable sum at that time—and was able to give his family a nice home and a comfortable life. Still, he wasn't satisfied.

In April of that year, Jerry quit his job as vice president of marketing at Wyatt Industries in Texas and opened his own company, but only after he had recruited Alvin Wilson, the best turnaround guy in the business. Jerry and Alvin founded Wilson Strickland. With the help of Pinky Miles, the manager of a Texas refinery, Jerry's start-up soon began acquiring jobs, smaller jobs at first and then larger jobs as he proved himself. Jim Robinson, a Wyatt engineer, soon joined Jerry's team.

Unfortunately, early on, Jerry had traded the controlling portion of his company to ChemShare for financing, and over the next few years, he realized that he had made a mistake. He did not have control and could not grow the company in the direction that he wanted. In 1981, Jim left Wilson Strickland to open his own company.

By 1982, Wilson Strickland was hundreds of thousands of dollars in debt, and ChemShare backed out, handing Jerry the floundering business. Jim's company, Altair Construction, was not doing well either, so the two companies merged to create AltairStrickland. Alvin retired and was replaced by Mike Walton.

Jerry, Jim, and Mike became known in industry as "the three amigos." Despite the huge problems they had to overcome in the beginning—meeting payroll, obtaining contracts, and hiring quality employees—the three men believed in each other and somehow managed to pull through by borrowing money against contracts to pay their workforce.

Jerry continued to drink, his way of bolstering his confidence. His position required that he entertain clients regularly, and much of his business was conducted over drinks at restaurants and strip clubs. Many deals for his company were brokered between cocktails and half-naked women dancing seductively on a pole.

While Jerry's professional life was slowly but steadily improving, his home life was falling apart. Jimmie Lee didn't like Jerry's drinking, but Jerry didn't think he had a problem. "I never thought I was drunk," he said. "I had never had a DUI or an accident while driving drunk. There were no significant instances where I made bad mistakes. I only got really drunk about three times per year."

Jerry thought if he could remember what he had done the previous night, he did not have a problem. He gave himself a test each morning, just to be sure. He and Jimmie Lee began having terrible fights, and their children began having problems as a result.

"There was a lot of misery in my home," he said. "There were a lot of verbal fights our neighbors could hear."

Chip, Patia, and Whitney began to react. Chip began drinking and using drugs. Patia also escaped into alcohol, and cocaine quickly became her drug of choice. Whitney went wild, his escapades often landing him a night in the drunk tank or in a ditch. Only Carter, the youngest and most introspective, seemed to develop coping skills and managed to escape his family's predilection for addiction.

Jerry, always wrapped up in his business, was never there, and Jimmie Lee, who was dealing with her own issues with prescription medication, became angrier and angrier. In 1986, she demanded that Jerry attend a workshop hosted by John Bradshaw, a self-help practitioner.

"You will go," she said.

Jerry argued at first, but he went.

On the first day of the workshop, Jerry explained to the attendees all seated in a circle that he had four children, three of whom were using drugs and alcohol. "I want to know how to fix them," he said.

On the second day, he was given an assignment: If he dreamed that night, he was to try to remember the dream and report back the next day. That night, Jerry saw the horses battling for supremacy.

He returned the next day and described his dream. Therapists at the workshop translated it for Jerry. "The horses represented my good side and my dark side, each battling to win control. My wife and children were the pine trees, standing there watching, wondering what was going to happen. That struck a chord with me. By the end of the workshop, I realized I was an alcoholic. I knew I had to change my life if I wanted my children to recover from their addictions."

That Sunday, Jerry went to his office and left a note for his partners: "I'm an alcoholic. I'm going to Sierra Tucson to get sober. I will do what I can from afar. Here are a couple of signed checks to carry you through. If you need more, you can reach me in Arizona. I will be back in a month."

Jerry flew to Tucson, Arizona. A van picked him up and transported him to Sierra Tucson late Sunday night. "When I arrived, I saw two mountain peaks ahead of us, like the ones I saw in my dream," Jerry said. "I knew then that I was in the right place."

While Jerry embraced the basic tenets of Alcoholics Anonymous, spiritually he began to move in a different direction. He became captivated by the nature-based spiritualism of Native Americans while listening intently to a guest speaker from the Ute Indian tribe, and he began to learn everything he could about Ute beliefs, customs, and culture. When he returned to Houston, he sought out a Native American spiritual guide to help him on his journey of discovery.

From the moment Jerry left the treatment facility, he did not touch another drop of alcohol. It was not easy. He could smell a glass of red wine from across a restaurant, but his resolve was strong. "The difference in me was pretty dramatic," he said. "I felt good physically. There were no more hangovers. I became more confident and was so much more self-aware. I left Tucson determined to find my good side. Both of my horses were going to be white. In my business, I cut out all of the drinking and entertainment. I learned that the best way to close a deal is through honesty and integrity. Our company grew because people respected that."

Jerry had fixed himself, but he couldn't fix his marriage, and he and Jimmie Lee divorced. He turned his attention to his children. He knew that he had made many promises to them he had not kept. Business had always been his number one priority. He hoped to become a role model and began trying to find ways to help them.

By this time, Jerry had sent Patia to California to live with her aunt with the hope that a new environment would help her. It did. Patia changed her life after joining Narcotics Anonymous.

Whitney, who worked with his father, was more problematic. After numerous incidents that involved arrests and car wrecks, Jerry practiced tough love and told his son that he was done with him if he didn't quit drinking. Eventually, Whitney got help, but he would have to hit rock bottom first.

In 1987, Jerry was blindsided with a tragedy for which there was no cure.

His oldest son, Chip, who for much of his life had assumed the role of parent to his brothers and sister, was diagnosed with AIDS. Jerry had known for three years that Chip was gay. He had uncovered his son's secret one evening after Chip borrowed his car. "I found a magazine in my car that listed the gay bars and gay bath houses in Houston," Jerry recalled. "We went to lunch one day, and he admitted that he was gay. When he told me, I couldn't swallow. I couldn't breathe."

Chip asked Jerry to read a particular book about homosexuality, and Jerry agreed. He read the book and gained some understanding, enough to accept his son's sexual preferences without anger or judgment. Chip eventually went to the PRIDE Institute in Minneapolis, Minnesota, to overcome his drug and alcohol addictions, and he, like his father, was successful. Jerry, Whitney, and Carter went to visit Chip during family week, and it was there that Jerry began to get a real understanding about the problems with which many homosexuals suffer. By the time Chip introduced Jerry to his partner, Steve Kubenka, Jerry was able to give Steve a chance. Over time, he began to see that love comes in many varieties, and he and Steve became friends and then family.

One day, Chip came down with a bronchial infection, and Jerry visited him in the hospital. When he walked in, Jerry wondered what the sign on the door meant.

"Dad, they told me I have AIDS," Chip said, tearing up.

In those days, no one really knew anything about the disease.

"Well, what can we do? What do the doctors say?" Jerry asked, devastated and in shock.

There was nothing anyone could do, but for Jerry, that had not yet sunk in. He learned about a doctor in Houston who used a drug that seemed to be helping. He sent his son to the doctor in hopes that he could be cured.

Chip, now sober like Patia and Whitney, watched his diet and followed his doctor's orders. With Jerry's help, he soon opened a funky gift shop in Austin, Texas, which became quite popular among locals and tourists. He tried to live his life to the fullest, aware that each moment would count.

Jerry bought a family lake house forty minutes from Austin. Three out of four weekends each month, he would drive there on Friday to spend the weekend with Chip, Steve, and some of their friends. Chip celebrated his passion for gourmet cooking by creating elaborate meals with his father. The two men became closer than ever. Those weekends would sustain Jerry through the nightmare of losing his oldest child.

On November 5, 1994, at the age of thirty-six, Chip's compromised immune system succumbed to a bout of pneumonia. His death was hard on everyone—the sister who he had loved so much, the brothers who had looked up to him for guidance, and Jerry, who had spent the past eight years spending every moment he could with his son.

"My children and I spent a lot of quality time together during this time," Jerry said. "Chip's illness brought the whole family together."

Eighteen months after Chip passed away, medical breakthroughs made living with AIDS possible. It was too late for Chip, but Steve, who was diagnosed with HIV later, survived and remains a member of the Strickland family.

In Chip's honor, Jerry helped the Out Youth organization in Austin open a library named after his son, and he donated one thousand books that would increase understanding about homosexuality.

During Chip's illness, Jerry began to seek relief from the despair he felt as he watched his son weaken. His search for peace and truth led him to Dr. William Taegel, a shamanic guide who conducted sweat lodge sessions. Jerry entered the sweat lodge the first time not knowing what to expect. He certainly didn't expect to find the love of his life, Linda Rothbauer, known as Peace Flower to members of Taegel's tribe.

At first, Linda was not interested in the good-looking, single businessman. After numerous random encounters over a period of months, Jerry finally asked her to go on a date with him. Linda had been single for twenty-five years and had no desire to get married, but Jerry poured on the charm. It took him a while to convince her, but in April 1996, they were married. In Linda, Jerry found complete understanding and lasting love, and he welcomed a new addition to his family, Linda's son, Steven.

Through the years, Jerry had struggled to keep AltairStrickland solvent. By the very nature of the work, turnarounds are stressful, but Jerry experienced setback after setback. In 1984, the Charter Company declared bankruptcy. At the time, the refinery owed Jerry $450,000. It took years to get paid. In the meantime, AltairStrickland barely held on. That story was repeated in different ways many times over the years, but Jerry persevered. Then, in 1996, AltairStrickland employees began experiencing skin and lung problems while working at a refinery in El Paso, Texas. The $4 million job was shut down, AltairStrickland refused to allow its employees to work in an unsafe environment. The refinery hired another company to complete the job.

AltairStrickland sued, assuming the tremendous cost of legal fees that were required to go up against a major player with unlimited funds. Jerry soon found himself weighted with an incredible burden. The company had to stay afloat. Jerry and his partners' refusal to back down in the face of surmounting debt led to an astonishing verdict—$87 million. Realizing that an appeal could erase the award, AltairStrickland settled for $10 million, but that put Jerry back in the black.

Soon he began spreading the wealth. Jerry helped several of his employees set up companies, including Mike Jeansonne, who opened The Turnaround Management Company, and Eddie Garza, who opened Turnaround Welding Services. Other companies followed, and while Jerry made money from these ventures, some of his employees also became millionaires.

By 2002, AltairStrickland had been in business for twenty-five years. The three amigos had weathered many storms together, but their perseverance had paid off. In 2004 and 2005, hurricanes Ivan, Katrina, and Rita damaged many refineries along the Gulf Coast. Suddenly AltairStrickland was overwhelmed with new contracts. At the height of their success, the partners decided to sell.

Jerry came up with a plan to sell only sixty-nine percent of the company, which would allow the partners to still enjoy some of the fruit of their labor. AltairStrickland sold for approximately $190 million, and the partners still owned thirty-one percent. Jerry stayed on as chairman of the board. AltairStrickland soon merged with another company, Repcon, and a new corporation, RepconStrickland, was formed.

In 2008, Jerry was diagnosed with idiopathic pulmonary fibrosis, a condition that inhibits the lungs from performing correctly. His prognosis was not good— three- to-five years. Although Linda had taught him to be open about everything in their marriage, for the next six months, Jerry couldn't bring himself to tell her this dreadful news. When he finally revealed the truth, Linda and Jerry decided that they would not accept the prognosis. Jerry enrolled in a research program at the University of Miami, where he received regular infusions of bone marrow stem cells. "Stem cells delay the progress of scar tissue buildup," Jerry explained. "I still have to get injections every six months."

Seven years after the initial sale of AltairStrickland, EMCOR Group bought RepconStrickland for almost a half-billion dollars. Due to Jerry's vision, he and his partners received thirty-one percent of the selling-price.

At seventy-seven years old, Jerry officially retired. All of his hard work had paid off beyond his wildest dreams, but Jerry wasn't finished working yet. He simply switched directions.

"I feel like it's important to be a role model," Jerry said. "We're involved with some really good charities. When I was growing up, everybody helped one another, and I've impressed it upon my family that we must continue that tradition. I remember reading about a man who lived in a boxcar. When he knocked on the doors of poor families, they would give him food. When he knocked on the doors of rich families, they shunned him. I know how hard it is to be poor. My life and my family are about helping people."

To that end, Jerry has become involved with numerous charities, including The Wheelhouse, an organization that helps men who are addicted to drugs and alcohol. He and Linda created The Linda and Jerry Strickland Family Foundation, which provides each of their children with $45,000 per year to give to the charity of their choice. Linda and Jerry also donated money to Camp Aranzazu, a seventy-acre camp for disabled children, located in Rockport, Texas, to build a large pavilion that now serves as the camp's activities center.

"We're developing marine biology and fishing camp facilities, and we're building more and more cabins for children on dialysis. Whitney's entire family works at Camp Aranzazu one week every year. It's a neat place," Jerry said.

The couple also provided the seed money to establish Extra Special People, a camp for kids in Athens, Georgia. "The camp started with $80,000, and its operating budget has grown to a half-million dollars," Jerry said. "We have $2 million in our capital fund to help us design a world-class camp for these kids."

Jerry says everyone in his family donates their time and resources to smaller charities in an effort to make the biggest impact. His thirteen grandchildren are being raised to understand the importance of giving and to continue their parents' work. "It's all about breaking the cycle," Jerry said. "It's not about what we do for ourselves. It's about how we help in the evolution of goodness for the future."

Jerry's desire that his family will continue in that tradition prompted him to set up a college trust for his grandchildren, contingent upon each of them performing one hundred sixty hours of community service during their high school years. His forethought is already working. His son Carter worked at a camp for the blind while in high school. Carter's oldest son, Owen, worked at the Extra Special People camp one year, and the next year, he went to Hawaii to build shelters for people in need.

Patia and her daughters Taylor and Megan are involved with the Phoenix Center in Marble Falls, Texas, which provides therapy for children traumatized by abuse. In 2015, one hundred seventy-one children attended the summer camp. Patia and her daughters spent several weeks there working with the children.

Jerry sometimes wishes that he would have been a better parent to his children when they were young. He wishes he had been the parents that his children have become, but as he looks at them today, as he witnesses all that Patia, Whitney, Carter, and his stepson, Steven, do for others, and what their children now do, Jerry smiles.

His heart is full.

"Everything means something. If you throw a rock into a stream, the rock will sink to the bottom, but the ripples will keep flowing. I was once that rock at the bottom of the stream. When I got sober, I learned to trust myself and began to live my life with integrity. My integrity drew people to me, people who succeeded and then shared their resources to help others," Jerry said. "Because I changed, my children also changed, breaking the cycle of addiction. My children and grandchildren now dedicate their lives to helping others. My sobriety and the lessons I learned created a ripple effect that has helped change the lives of hundreds of people. It only takes one person to start a chain reaction. Pay it forward. That's the best advice I can give."

It has now been six years since Jerry was diagnosed and given three- to-five years to live. He is beating the odds as he has always done, and he's not finished yet. He still has so much life to live and so much love to give.

For more information, please visit www.outyouth.org, www.camparanzazu.org, www.phoenixcentertexas.org, or www.extraspecialpeople.com.

WHITNEY STRICKLAND

CRASH AND BURN—THE LONG ROAD TO REDEMPTION

"It was like being in a car with the gas pedal slammed down to the floor and nothing to do but hold on and pretend to have some semblance of control. But control was something I'd lost a long time ago."

—Nic Sheff, author

T he sound of a Hot Pockets sandwich hitting the concrete floor startled him to consciousness. Whitney Strickland shook his head to clear it. The steel bars told him he was in jail, but he couldn't remember how he had gotten there. He closed his eyes, praying that he had not wrecked another vehicle. The memories began coming in bursts.

Caroline had taken the kids out of town on Friday.

He had been drunk all weekend.

Sunday morning, he had gone sailing with his friend, Ava, on her sailboat.

He had crashed the sailboat into a shrimp boat, slamming the shrimp boat into the Kemah boardwalk.

After that, they had gone to several bars. Whitney had ended up at Lipsticks, a strip club where he had run up a $300 tab. The last things he remembered were two rum and cokes on the bar in front of him and two dancers on each side of him.

Then he woke up in jail.

A guard soon brought him to booking, where a police officer found Whitney's Alcoholics Anonymous chip in his wallet. The officer informed him that he had been charged with driving while intoxicated. Whitney grinned sheepishly. "Sometimes I'm on the wagon, and sometimes I fall off," he said.

Whitney called his wife, Caroline, who brought their children to visit him and then left. His mother, Jimmie Lee, paid his bail, but she didn't stick around to give him a ride home.

A few hours later, Whitney was released. He thought about calling his father, Jerry, but he knew better. Realizing that no one would come to pick him up, he began to walk home. As he crossed the bridge over the boardwalk, so many thoughts ran through his mind. He felt horrible that his children had seen him like that.

He felt horrible about a lot of things.

I've been to treatment centers. I've talked to psychiatrists. I've done everything. I'm dying a long, slow death. I'll just jump off this bridge and get it over with.

Whitney put his foot on the rail.

Whitney Strickland was born in Boston in 1968, the third child of Jimmie Lee and Jerry Strickland. As a young boy, he loved anything that had wheels—his tricycle, his Green Machine, his electric car. Every day, he zoomed up and down the sidewalk in front of his home, enjoying the feeling of power that riding fast gave him.

When he was six years old, his family moved to Houston. Back then his childhood was picture-perfect. His family lived in a nice subdivision. He loved his older brother, Chip; his older sister, Patia; and his little brother, Carter. His mother threw extravagant birthday parties and invited all of their friends. "When I was little, everything looked pretty good," Whitney said.

By the time he was ten, Whitney's home life had changed dramatically. His father worked long hours to take care of the family, and he was never home. Jimmie Lee was depressed and sometimes stayed locked in her room for days. Patia began taking care of her brothers, fixing them pancakes for dinner and making sure they took their baths before bedtime.

When Jerry was home, he and Jimmie Lee fought constantly. "I remember one time they were fighting in the kitchen," Whitney said. "They threw flour all over each other, and my mom came to my room covered in it. She told me everything was okay, but that was pretty scary for a ten-year-old. I often took off on my bike to get away from the house when they were both there."

The fights between Jerry and Jimmie Lee escalated over a period of years. Even when he was outside, Whitney could hear them screaming at each other. So could the neighbors.

Whitney knew that his father liked to drink, and he soon began to sneak into Jerry's liquor cabinet. Then he found Jerry's hidden supply in the garage. He availed himself of that, as well.

"Chip and Patia were already doing drugs by this time," Whitney said. "I started drinking and smoking weed when I was twelve."

Up to that point, Whitney had always been a good child, respectful of his parents and others, but alcohol, from the very beginning, brought out his destructive side. "When I was thirteen, I was arrested for shooting out some windows at the high school," he said. "At fifteen, I was arrested for public intoxication and stealing lawn art. I once stole a Santa Claus out of someone's yard."

During high school, Whitney often snuck away for lunch to get high and drink beer. As he got older, he became more and more out of control. No one in his home paid too much attention. Patia and Chip were living in their own drug-filled worlds. Jimmie Lee had become more depressed and had developed an addiction to pills. Jerry was preoccupied with business.

The day he got his driver's license, Whitney asked his mother if he could borrow her car to attend a prayer meeting. She said, "yes." There was no prayer meeting. Whitney got high and then smashed Jimmie Lee's Mercedes into someone's house.

One day, when Whitney was seventeen, he cooked up some ketamine—an animal tranquilizer, called "Special K" by users—and handed a matchbox filled with the drug to a friend. The boy sniffed it all, hopped in his car, and drove away. "The principal and the police pulled me out of class," Whitney said. "They told me the boy was in the hospital, and the only thing he had said was my name. Fortunately, he was okay." The police could not determine what drugs the boy had used, so no charges were filed.

During this time, Jerry realized he had a problem with alcohol and went to Sierra Tucson for help. Whitney attended family week at the treatment center and received an intervention. Soon after, Jimmie Lee and Jerry separated. Whitney chose to live with his father. Father and son attended Alcoholics Anonymous (AA) meetings together, encouraging each other every step of the way. Jerry had high hopes for his son's future, but because he was so young, Whitney had a difficult time relating to the other men at AA. He stayed sober for one year and graduated from high school.

Whitney enrolled at the University of Houston and moved in with an old friend. "I started drinking again, and a week into college, I wrecked my car," he said. "A few weeks later, I got a DUI."

When he wasn't in school, Whitney worked for his father in different capacities. He was a boilermaker, a pipefitter, a craftsman. "I made good money, but that just allowed me to drink more," he said.

Despite his addictions, Whitney made decent grades. Soon he was accepted at the University of Texas and moved to Austin. There, he indulged even more. "I had a homeless guy living with me, and all we did was drink," Whitney said.

While at a bar one evening, Whitney met a girl who liked to drink as much as he did. Caroline was British, and Whitney traveled to England and Scotland with her. "I loved it. They really know how to drink there," he said. "I brought Caroline back to the States, and we got married."

Before long, Whitney dropped out of college because he couldn't remember where his classes were located. He began working turnarounds and traveling all over the southern United States. When his daughter, Aubrey, was born, he brought his family with him to each job location.

Turnarounds are seasonal, so Whitney didn't work during the summer months. "I should have tried to get a job, but I thought I would just sit on my porch and drink beer while Caroline worked. I drank like a fish," he said.

Sometimes he thought about quitting. One time, when he was working a turnaround in Decatur, Alabama, Whitney realized that his payroll check was not accurate. He called his boss to complain. "I had been drinking for four or five days straight," he said. "I don't know what happened after that phone call. I woke up in my truck in Jackson, Mississippi."

Whitney drove home, worried about the blackout. He knew he had a problem, and he wanted to stop, but that would not prove to be easy. When he got home, he told Caroline what had happened. Her response was, "I've got a six-pack in the refrigerator. Get a beer."

He got a beer.

Whitney soon went to work in Texas City, his good intentions all but forgotten. "I worked seven days each week, twelve hours per day as a supervisor, and I got off work around seven each evening. I would drink until one or two in the morning; go to Jack in the Box for a triple meat cheeseburger, curly fries, and a Dr. Pepper; sleep an hour or two; and get to the gate by five. When I got off work, I'd start drinking again."

Although there can be no excuses, there were contributing factors. Whitney was very close to his older brother, Chip. When he learned that Chip had been diagnosed with AIDS, he was devastated. Barring a miracle, Whitney knew what was going to happen, and he simply couldn't handle it. He did what he had always done. He climbed inside a bottle and hid from life.

When his son, Angus, was born, Whitney decided that he needed to spend more time with his children. He took a job in human resources at his father's company that required he work only forty hours per week. "Now I had more time to drink," he said. "Between drinking and hangovers, there wasn't much quality time with my kids."

One night, while he was out celebrating a coworker's birthday, Whitney wrecked his company truck on the way home. "I closed the bar, and then rolled the truck three or four times. I was thrown through the passenger window. There was so much blood that the police thought I was dead," he said.

Whitney was rushed to the hospital, where he lay on a gurney with his head split open. To his right, police wrote tickets. To his left, several AA members waited to talk with him. At the foot of the gurney, Caroline pulled another woman's jewelry out of his pants pockets.

"You'd think I would quit drinking," Whitney said. "I really tried sometimes. I went in and out of AA every year, whining about my cuts and bruises and trying to make everyone happy."

Whitney stopped drinking several times, but then he'd start up again. Once, after he had been sober for a while, he picked up a twelve-pack on his way home. When Caroline saw him sitting on the porch with a beer, she said. "I don't care if you drink yourself to death as long as you do it with me."

That disturbed him.

Then in 2000, Caroline went out of town. While she was gone, Whitney wrecked a sailboat, drank till he blacked out, went to jail, and stood with his foot on the railing of the boardwalk over Galveston Bay.

He wanted to die.

Whitney took a deep breath and was preparing to jump when suddenly he saw a very bright light in the distance. "It was a perfect light," he said. "A light full of hope. Looking at the light, I realized I could be a great man if I could just quit drinking."

Whitney took his foot off the railing.

His spirit renewed, he walked several miles to his house. For the first time in so long, he had hope. When he got there, he was shocked to find all of his personal possessions scattered across the front yard. Caroline had thrown him out.

After a few minutes, Whitney convinced her to let him come inside. It took a day and a half to recover from the effects of the alcohol he had consumed. As soon as his hangover dissipated, Whitney went straight to an AA meeting, determined he was going to beat his addiction. This time he got a sponsor, but his road to sobriety wasn't easy.

Caroline and Whitney split up. His driver's license was revoked. The passenger window in his truck was broken out. His clothes were piled up in the backseat of the truck. He had no money and lived in a twenty-dollar-per-night motel. "My dad wouldn't help me. He had been practicing tough love for a while by now. My sister was also sober, and I knew she wasn't going to help me. My mom was a pill addict. Chip was gone. I had to do this on my own."

For Whitney, success came through listening to his sponsor and practicing the twelve steps, and through service to others. In the beginning, he developed panic attacks, but he prayed and meditated his way through those. The Up the Street Club, a twelve-step recovery club, helped him tremendously. There, he painted walls, filled soft drink and candy machines, mopped floors, and performed any menial task that was required.

Whitney began to get well. Despite going through a divorce and custody battle, he stayed sober. He dedicated himself to his children, determined to make amends for the mistakes he had made.

A year went by.

Slowly, his relationship with his father improved. Pleased with the effort Whitney was making, Jerry gave him more responsibility in the company. "We worked together really well," Whitney said. "I could think what he thought before he thought it. He had vision, and I implemented his vision."

In his second year of sobriety, Whitney began dating Tisha, a woman he had hired at AltairStrickland. He had once worked for her father. The two fell in love and were married in 2003. Whitney became a stepfather to her son, Christopher. This marriage was much different from his last. The foundation was strong, based on love, respect, and Christian principles. For the first time since he had been very young, Whitney was genuinely happy.

He continued to go to AA meetings and soon became president of the board of directors of the Up the Street Club. He found that he enjoyed helping others find their way to a better life through sobriety.

By 2006, Whitney's life had completely turned around in only six years. He had been promoted to chief marketing officer and human resources director at Altair-Strickland, and through his work at the company, he became a millionaire. He also discovered a new cause.

"A man named Walter Hall invited me to a board meeting at The Wheelhouse in Deer Park, Texas," Whitney explained. "I was impressed when he showed me the inner workings of the organization, so I joined the board and got really involved."

The Wheelhouse, often referred to as "the last house on the block," is an alcohol and drug addiction treatment facility for men only. "When a man gets to The Wheelhouse, he's been through other places, his family is sick of him, and he has nowhere else to go," Whitney said.

Founded in 1952, The Wheelhouse has a very high success rate because of its unique model. Many of the men who go through the live-in, bare-bones program return to help the next round of men recover. There is no charge to the men or to their families.

The program is intense—thirty days with no television, radio, Internet access, or telephone calls. Meetings are held at 7:00 a.m., 1:00 p.m., and 8:00 p.m. The men are allowed only two books to study, the *Big Book* (AA's textbook), and the dictionary. Within five days, they must choose a sponsor.

After thirty days, the men move to a three-quarter house for ninety days, where they pay a small weekly rental and are required to get a job. They must continue to attend meetings at The Wheelhouse.

When the program is completed, the men are free to go about their lives, armed with the tools they need to remain sober and productive.

"As I learned how the program works, I started putting two and two together," Whitney said. "At AltairStrickland, we were always in need of construction workers, and these were sober men who needed good jobs. It was a terrific way to help them and the company."

Ten years later, Whitney still serves on the board of directors at The Wheelhouse. He and his family are also involved with Camp Aranzazu, a camp for children with special needs. For one week every June, Whitney, Tisha, Christopher, Aubrey, and Angus go to this one-of-a-kind camp in Rockport, Texas, to wash dishes, clean toilets, and teach archery and canoeing to the children.

Like his father, Whitney believes that helping others is essential, an important part of growing as a person. "I made so many mistakes. I wrecked cars, motorcycles, boats. I was in and out of jail. I wrecked my life any way I could. Then I saw that light, and everything changed."

Whitney says that beating alcoholism is something a person has to choose to do on his or her own. "My best advice is to go to a twelve-step program to get the help you need. Families cannot help an alcoholic when he gets into trouble because it only prolongs the disease. Being honest is important. Alcohol causes brain damage in some people, and they don't have the capacity to be honest about their addiction. You have to evaluate what's really going on so that the proper help is offered."

The road to sobriety was a long and perilous one for Whitney. Of all of the Strickland children—with the exception of Carter, who managed to avoid the pitfalls of alcohol and drug use—Whitney was the last to recover.

"Being able to help my kids is my biggest accomplishment," he said. "Through my own mistakes, I gained a lot of knowledge that I can pass on to them, but it's an accidental accomplishment. Despite what they went through when they were young, they are great kids."

Today, Whitney, who has not touched a drop of alcohol in sixteen years, tries to be that perfect light that once saved him, not only for his children, but also for so many men who struggle with the disease of alcoholism.

For more information, please visit www.thewheelhouseinc.com.

DEENA BURNETT BAILEY

Surviving 9/11—the story of a hero's family

"Grief can destroy you—or focus you. You can decide a relationship was all for nothing if it had to end in death, and you alone. Or you can realize that every moment of it had more meaning than you dared to recognize at the time, so much meaning it scared you, so you just lived, just took for granted the love and laughter of each day, and didn't allow yourself to consider the sacredness of it.

But when it's over and you're alone, you begin to see it wasn't just a movie and a dinner together, not just watching sunsets together, not just scrubbing a floor or washing dishes together or worrying over a high electric bill. It was everything. It was the why of life, every event and precious moment of it. The answer to the mystery of existence is the love you shared sometimes so imperfectly, and when the loss wakes you to the deeper beauty of it, to the sanctity of it, you can't get off your knees for a long time, you're driven to your knees not by the weight of the loss but by gratitude for what preceded the loss. And the ache is always there, but one day not the emptiness, because to nurture the emptiness, to take solace in it, is to disrespect the gift of life."

—Dean Koontz, *Odd Hours*

Deena Burnett got up early that morning to cook breakfast for her children. The twins, Halley and Madison, had started kindergarten the week before, and this was to be Anna Clare's first day of preschool. Deena smiled as she set the table, listening to the girls giggling excitedly.

Hers was a great life. Deena and her husband, Tom, had been married nine years and were still very much in love. On this morning, Tom was scheduled to ring the opening bell at the New York Stock Exchange on Wall Street—a reward for a David and Goliath-style merger he and his boss had masterminded.

While she cooked, Deena turned on the news and watched an airplane crash into the North Tower of the World Trade Center in New York City. In those early moments, information was sketchy. Deena listened as newscasters speculated about what kind of plane had hit the tower and whether it was an accident. Deena kept her eye on the television while the girls ate their breakfast.

Then a second plane hit the South Tower.

Deena's mother called.

"Tom's fine. He's scheduled on a later flight," Deena told her.

Tom's mother called. "Have you talked to Tom?" she said, her voice laced with worry.

"He's fine," Deena reassured her.

Deena didn't know that Tom had changed his plans. He had been traveling for three weeks with only a six-hour visit home the previous Friday. Eager to get back to his family, he asked his boss and best friend, Keith, to ring the bell at the Stock Exchange.

Tom hurried to Newark Airport and boarded United Flight 93.

━━━

Deena Burnett Bailey grew up in Halley, Arkansas, a small farming community sparsely populated with sixty-three people. Her parents, Donald and Sandra Burchfield, worked hard and made sacrifices to give Deena and her younger brother, Scotty, a good life in what was one of the poorest areas of the country. Everyone in the town knew each other, and Deena's grandparents, aunts, uncles, and cousins all lived nearby. Because this was a tight-knit community, it was not uncommon to get your hand or bottom smacked by a relative or neighbor if you did something wrong.

"It was a village raising all of the children who lived there," Deena said. "Anyone might be watching, so we minded our Ps and Qs all the time."

By Halley standards, the Burchfields were upper middle class. Donald was a cotton farmer, and Sandra was a registered nurse. Deena grew up taking ballet and piano lessons, participating in sports, and attending a private school some twenty miles away. She was a good student, excelling in everything except math.

Then her parents divorced. Although divorce is typical today, back then it was unchartered territory and fodder for gossip throughout the community. Sandra remarried seven months after the divorce, and Donald remarried within two years. Through her father's marriage, Deena gained a two-year-old stepsister, Kristen, whom she loved dearly, but the adjustment to her new way of life was difficult for the teenaged girl.

"My brother and I were shuttled between two households of blended families," Deena said. "We were very aware that neither of these families liked one another. We were careful about answering questions that pertained to our parents and our new families. We tried not to fuel the fire between our parents with information we shared. The feeling was one of not belonging—just always being a guest in a house that used to feel like home. We knew without a doubt we were loved, but the dissent between my mom and dad was blatant. It was unsettling."

After her graduation from high school, Deena enrolled in Northeast Louisiana University in Monroe, Louisiana, where she majored in broadcast journalism. She wanted to be a news reporter. When she earned her degree, she got a job at a radio station in Fort Walton Beach, Florida. "The pay wasn't very good, so I supplemented my income by waiting tables," she said.

Deena worked at the radio station for a year and a half and then lost her job because there was not enough advertising revenue to pay her salary. She realized that the profession she had chosen was volatile, so she decided to work with her mother at an adult congregate living facility Sandra owned. Sandra, who had always dreamed of being a flight attendant, often suggested that Deena might enjoy doing that. It had never been Deena's ambition, but after several years spent working one job during the day and then waiting tables at night, she began to consider it.

In 1988, Deena started a three-month training period with Continental Airlines. "I went through training and got stationed out of New York. Two weeks after I reported for duty, I got a notice that there might be a layoff," she said. Employees at Eastern Airlines had gone on strike, and Continental and Eastern were under the same corporate umbrella. Because of the uncertainty, she began applying at other airlines.

Deena went to work for Delta Airlines in April 1989 and soon began traveling the world—Ireland, Germany, Hong Kong, Alaska, Hawaii, and every small town in the southern United States. It was not unusual for her to have a two- or three-day layover on international flights, so she was able to explore foreign countries on her days off. "I loved it. I absolutely loved it," she said. "I got to meet so many people, and every day was different. One day, you might be called in to work at two in the morning, and another day, you're coming home at that time. It was always exciting."

Deena was stationed in Atlanta, Georgia. One evening in July, she and some friends went to a bar in a hotel near her apartment for happy hour. Deena's friend, Camille, struck up a conversation with a man at the bar and invited him to follow them to another bar. Deena was a little irritated because she and her girlfriends were supposed to be having a girls' night, and she didn't like the idea of a strange man tagging along.

At the next bar, when Camille completely ignored the man, Deena began to feel sorry for him.

"I'm Deena," she told him, smiling.

"Tom Burnett," he said, smiling bigger.

As they talked, Deena realized that this good-looking man was very charming and nice. Before they left, Camille wrote down the names and phone numbers of all of the girls in their group on a piece of paper and handed it to Tom. A week later, he called Camille and left her a message, inviting Camille and Deena to a barbecue. Camille didn't return his call. Deena thought that was rude.

"You should call him," she urged Camille.

"You should call him," Camille said.

Deena called Tom and told him she wouldn't be comfortable going to his apartment alone. He asked if she would meet him at Applebee's. Deena said yes. At the restaurant, they talked for hours, and then Tom asked her for another date.

Two weeks later, Deena told her mother that she was going to marry him.

"Are you in love with him?" Sandra asked.

"No, but I'm going to be," Deena responded.

Tom was in the process of moving to Atlanta from St. Louis, Missouri. He had recently been hired as the eastern regional manager for Calcitek, a company that sold dental implants. Deena lived a block from the hotel where he was staying. Theirs would not be a usual romance because they both traveled so much.

"Because of my job, I could travel to wherever he was to spend time with him," Deena said. "Sometimes he would surprise me and show up on one of my flights. Other times, our dates were the flights. If he had to go to Boston, I'd get on the flight, have dinner with him, and then fly back to Atlanta. We romanced each other in the air."

Although they had talked about marriage since early in the relationship, Tom didn't formally propose for two years. Then one day, Deena went to his apartment and found a picture of Tom and a female co-worker. "It seemed very friendly to me, so I called him at work," she said. "He knew I was mad, and he rushed home with a bottle of champagne."

Tom pulled out three boxes, each containing a ring that resembled the kind that come from bubblegum machines.

"Pick one," he said.

Deena was still mad, but she picked one.

"Will you marry me?" Tom said.

Deena didn't respond.

"I'm not going to ask you twice," Tom said.

"Yes," Deena said, looking at the plastic ring on her finger. "Does this mean we're engaged?"

In the past, friends had often told Tom that he wasn't a romantic guy. "He wasn't," Deena said. "He thought his proposal was hilarious."

Six weeks before their wedding shower, Tom bought Deena a real engagement ring, and on April 25, 1992, the couple wed in a Catholic church just ten miles from the small township where Deena grew up.

Their romance in the air continued. Deena would sometimes find out what flight Tom was on and leave notes at the gate for him. When he arrived at the airport she had just left, the gate agent would give him her note. They traded notes across the country and talked on the phone a lot.

"It was not uncommon for us to speak on the phone, even if it was just to say 'hi,' every hour, every day," Deena said. "It was the most significant element of our marriage. We learned to communicate well with each other. We talked about everything. Nothing was off limits. We were so good at saying what we really thought that we could make instant adjustments in our behavior. I could say, 'I need you to not do that,' and he would stop, and vice versa."

While they had many things in common—their faith in God, strong family backgrounds, similar morals and virtues—their personalities were very different. "Tom was intense; I was not," Deena said. "He liked being in the foreground; I liked being in the background. He had a large personality and was witty and very intelligent. He was a mathematician, an athlete, a poet, a carpenter. He could sing and play piano. He was whoever he needed to be at any moment, and he could do anything. He really was a Renaissance man. I was not nearly as complex as he was."

Deena, on the other hand, was shy, quiet, a people pleaser. She preferred listening to speaking. She was a dreamer, a follower, a hard worker. She never wanted to be the center of attention. She was a simple farm girl, but more adventurous than most.

Their differences only enhanced their marriage, and before long, they began trying to have children. However, Deena had difficulty conceiving. Finally, after the use of fertility drugs, she became pregnant. She and Tom were ecstatic.

Two weeks after she learned she was pregnant, Deena began bleeding. She called Tom, and he rushed home to take her to the doctor.

As the doctor administered the ultrasound, she asked incredulously, "How many are you having?"

"How many are in there?" Tom asked.

"One, two, three," the doctor counted. "Wait, the third one isn't developing, so two."

Deena had always wanted to have twins, and she and Tom excitedly began preparing for their babies to arrive. Deena took maternity leave and never went back to work as a flight attendant. In May 1996, Halley and Madison were born. In February 1998, the family welcomed Anna Clare.

"Tom's sisters thought it was hilarious," Deena said. "Tom had always envisioned a house full of boys, and now he lived with four girls. The girls would say, 'Daddy, let's have a tea party,' and Tom would say, 'Let's play football.'"

The family did everything together, and Deena grew to respect her husband more than ever. She thought he was capable of anything because he had proved that to her over and over. He was a thinker, a problem-solver, and a great provider for his family. Deena enjoyed being a homemaker and dedicated her life to her husband and her girls.

When Tom was offered a position as the chief operating officer of Thoratec Laboratories Corp., a medical device company located in Pleasanton, California, the family moved to San Ramon, forty-five miles east of San Francisco. Tom's boss, Keith Grossman, was also his best friend. Tom couldn't have been happier. He decorated the shelves in his office with busts of Abraham Lincoln, Winston Churchill, and Theodore Roosevelt, and went to work figuring out how to minimize the size of titanium devices. Before long, Keith and Tom began to work on a merger between Thoratec and Thermo Cardiosystems. It was highly unusual for a smaller company to acquire a larger company, but Tom and Keith were determined, and in February 2001, the two companies merged.

"It was a big, big deal," Deena said. "An incredible feat."

Because Thoratec now had seven hundred employees, Tom's responsibilities required that he spend a lot of time in New York and Newark, New Jersey. For the next six months, Deena and Tom communicated mostly as they always had—by phone, sometimes talking for hours at night, sometimes saying a quick "hi" or "I miss you."

When Tom returned home on Friday, September 7, 2001, he was happy to see Deena and the children. He had been gone for three weeks. While he was away, Deena had made arrangements for them to visit a couple of houses in the area that were for sale. They wanted a larger home to accommodate their family.

"Come on, honey. It won't take long. We've got to go look at these houses while you're here," Deena said.

"I've only got six hours," Tom complained, upset because he missed Deena and the kids so much. He had planned a trip for that weekend to visit his parents in Minneapolis, Minnesota, and he was scheduled to leave at eleven that night.

"It won't take long," Deena promised.

Realizing she was right, Tom agreed to go. At one of the houses they visited, he accidentally set off the security alarm, which did nothing to improve his mood.

When they returned home, Tom asked Deena what they were having for dinner.

"I didn't have time to cook anything," she said. "We can have leftovers."

Tom ate dinner with his family, but he wasn't talking and laughing like he normally did. He was cranky and upset that he would have to catch another plane so soon.

After dinner, Deena went upstairs and put the children to bed.

Later, Tom apologized. "I'm sorry," he said. "I'm tired, and I don't want to leave you and the kids.'"

Deena smiled and kissed him before she went back upstairs to get ready for bed. She and Tom had been married nine years by this time, and she understood why he had been upset. She didn't like all the time they had spent apart since the merger, either.

When it was time for him to leave, Tom went upstairs to say goodbye.

"Be safe," Deena said. Normally, Tom didn't respond to that, although Deena said it each time he flew.

This time, he said, "You bet I will."

Then he went to the airport.

After spending the weekend with his parents, Tom flew to New York for a round of meetings on Monday. He and Keith had been invited to ring the opening bell at the New York Stock Exchange on Wall Street the next morning, but Tom was missing his family.

Tuesday morning, September 11, 2001, Tom asked Keith to go without him so he could catch an early flight home.

As Tom boarded United Flight 93, Deena began cooking breakfast. Then she turned on the television and saw the breaking news.

At 6:27 a.m. Pacific standard time (PST), Deena was on the phone with her mother-in-law when another caller beeped in.

"Hello," she said, clicking over.

"Deena," Tom said.

"Tom, are you okay?" Deena said.

"No. I'm not. I'm on an airplane that's been hijacked."

"Hijacked?" Deena said, trying to comprehend what he was saying.

"Yes. They knifed a guy." Tom said.

"A passenger?"

"Yes."

"Where are you? Are you in the air?" Deena asked.

"Yes. Yes. Just listen. Our airplane has been hijacked. It's United Flight 93 from Newark to San Francisco. We are in the air. The hijackers have already knifed a guy. One of them has a gun. They are telling us there's a bomb on board. Please call the authorities."

Tom hung up.

"I couldn't believe it," Deena said. "I called 9-1-1 and tried to explain that this was not one of the planes that had flown into the World Trade Center, but they seemed bewildered."

While Deena was still on the phone with 9-1-1, Tom called again at 6:34 a.m. (PST).

"Hello," she said.

"They're in the cockpit. The guy they knifed is dead," Tom said.

"He's dead?"

"Yes. I tried to help him, but I couldn't get a pulse."

"Tom, they are hijacking planes all up and down the East Coast. They're taking them and hitting designated targets. They've already hit both towers of the World Trade Center."

"They're talking about crashing this plane." Tom paused for a moment, collecting his thoughts. "Oh, my God. It's a suicide mission."

Deena could hear him telling someone what was happening.

"Who are you talking to?" she asked.

"My seatmate. Do you know which airline is involved?"

"No. They don't know if they're commercial airplanes or not. The news reporters are speculating cargo planes, private planes, and commercial. No one knows."

"How many?"

"They're not sure. At least three. Maybe more."

"Okay. Okay," Tom said, thinking aloud. "Do you know who is involved?"

"No," Deena said.

"We're turning back toward New York. We're going back to the World Trade Center," Tom said. "No. Wait. We're turning back the other way. We're going south."

"What do you see?"

"Just a minute. I'm looking. I don't see anything. We're over a rural area. It's just fields. I've gotta go."

Tom hung up the phone.

Deena began scribbling notes about what Tom said on a tablet at the top of her grocery list. By this time, the FBI was monitoring her phone.

"There were things I remembered months, even years later," she recalled. "I couldn't think clearly. The FBI later said there were three calls. According to my notes, there were four. My thoughts were disjointed. I wasn't connecting the dots. My mind was panicking, but I am always very calm in a crisis. My husband was on a plane, and planes were going into the World Trade Center, but I didn't connect that his plane was going to go into a building. I thought he would be okay."

At 6:37 a.m. (PST), American Airlines Flight 77 crashed into the Pentagon.

Deena stared at the television, the telephone still clutched in her hand. Terrified by what she was seeing, she began sobbing.

Then the phone rang. It was 6:45 a.m. (PST).

"Deena," Tom said.

"Tom, you're okay," Deena cried.

"No. I'm not," Tom said.

"They just hit the Pentagon," Deena said.

Tom repeated her words to the people around him.

"Okay. Okay. What else can you tell me?"

"They think five airplanes have been hijacked. One is still on the ground. They believe all of them are commercial planes. I haven't heard them say which airline, but all of them originated on the East Coast."

"Do you know who is involved?"

"No."

"What is the probability of them having a bomb on board? I don't think they have one. I think they're telling us that for crowd control."

"A plane can survive a bomb if it's in the right place," Deena said, her years as a flight attendant guiding her words.

"Did you call the authorities?" Tom asked.

"Yes," Deena said. "They didn't know anything about your plane."

"They're talking about crashing this plane into the ground. We have to do something. I'm putting a plan together."

"Who's helping you?" Deena asked.

"Different people. Several people. There's a group of us. Don't worry. I'll call you back."

Deena tried to remain calm. The girls were still eating breakfast. She didn't want to scare them.

The phone rang again at 6:54 a.m. (PST).

"Tom?" Deena said, relieved again.

"Hi. Anything new?"

"No."

"Where are the kids?" Tom asked.

"They're fine. They're sitting at the table having breakfast. They're asking to talk to you."

"Tell them I'll talk to them later," Tom said.

"I called your parents. They know your plane has been hijacked," Deena said.

"Oh, you shouldn't have worried them."

"They're okay. Mary and Martha are with them."

"Good." Tom was silent for a moment. Deena listened to him breathe. "We're waiting until we're over a rural area. We're going to take back the airplane," he finally said.

"No," Deena cried. "Sit down. Be still. Be quiet and don't draw attention to yourself." Delta Airlines had trained her to say those exact words.

"Deena, if they're going to crash this plane into the ground, we're going to do something."

"What about the authorities?" Deena asked.

"We can't wait for the authorities. I don't know what they could do anyway," Tom replied. "It's up to us. I think we can do it."

"What do you want me to do?" Deena asked.

"Pray, Deena. Just pray."

"I am."

"Don't worry. I'll be home for dinner. I may be late, but I'll be home," Tom promised.

"Okay."

Neither said a word for a moment, and then Deena said, "I love you."

"Don't worry, Deena. We're going to do something."

Tom hung up the phone.

Deena called a friend and asked her to take the girls to school.

A San Ramon police officer knocked at the door. The FBI had sent him to sit with her. When the children were gone, Deena waited by the phone for a while, but there were no more calls. She knew that the FBI would be arriving soon, so she excused herself and went upstairs to get dressed. She was worried, but her faith in Tom quashed the panic that threatened.

"He didn't say goodbye to me, so I know he didn't expect to fail," she said. "He didn't convey any doubts to me, so although I was concerned for his safety, I wasn't concerned for his life. I had that much faith in him. I had never seen him not succeed. I trusted him. He sounded okay, like 'I've got this.'"

When she finished getting dressed, Deena walked downstairs. A new police officer, Chris Stangle, had arrived, and he was staring at the television with a strange look on his face.

"What's wrong?" Deena asked.

"I think there's been another plane crash," he said.

Deena ran to the television and listened as newscasters said the words that would forever change her life. United Flight 93 had crashed into a coalfield in Shanksville, Pennsylvania. Forty-four people were on board.

Deena fell into the couch, crying.

"It was devastating," she said. "I was in shock and overwhelmed with grief. I was also so angry. I knew that if the plane had crashed, someone had not done what Tom had told them to do."

Soon the phone began ringing, over and over. The media filled the front yard.

Just as Deena was about to unplug the phone, it rang again.

It was an employee from Sears, calling about Deena's car, which had broken down forty-five miles away the day before. She had left the car there, and Tom had told her he would take care of it when he got home.

"You need to come get your car," the man said.

Deena was crying so hard she couldn't speak. Officer Stangle took the phone from her and explained the situation. The employees at Sears pooled their money and had the car towed to the Volvo dealership. Volvo fixed it at no cost and delivered it to Deena's home.

That was the first of so many acts of kindness that would help Deena get through this unspeakable tragedy.

"Keith and Thoratec were terrific," Deena said. "They took over the tasks that come with death. They sent employees over to help out. They bought groceries. They answered phone calls and letters. They sent thank you notes. They hired a nanny to help me with the kids. They continued to pay Tom's salary so that we could have an income. They filed the life insurance paperwork. They were a life-saver."

The Red Cross also offered its assistance during those first days after the crash.

Others weren't so kind. When the names of the passengers were released, some banks froze the bank accounts and credit cards of some of the victims. "For the first two weeks, I couldn't access our bank accounts or credit cards because Tom was the main signatory, and I was the secondary," Deena said. "It was a nightmare. We had money, but I couldn't access it because Tom did not have a will, and I did not have a death certificate yet."

In the days and weeks following the crash, Deena's life turned upside down. The media followed her everywhere and called constantly. The farm girl who hated the limelight was thrust into it to grieve very publicly for the man she loved. Halley, Madison, and Anna Clare kept her going.

"Every morning, I would lie in bed asking myself, 'Do I get up today or do I not?'" Deena said. "And then I would think, 'What would I want my daughters to do?' I knew no matter what happened, I had to take care of my kids. I prayed a lot. My faith in God really helped me. I focused on getting through each moment. And then I put one foot in front of the other over and over and over."

In that first year after Tom's death, Deena met a lot of widowed women. "They all seemed so hurt, so sad," Deena said. "I remember thinking I didn't want to be that way. I didn't want to raise my girls in a home without laughter. I wanted to teach my daughters that you don't have to become a victim."

She set an example for them by doing everything she could to honor their father's memory. She spoke proudly about him to the media. "Before I stepped in front of a microphone, I always said a prayer. I asked God to make sure my words were His words," she said.

As the months went by, Deena's quiet strength sustained her through her grief, but her anger grew. She kept hearing Tom's words over and over, "Don't worry. We're going to do something." Since the morning of 9/11, she had been requesting that the FBI release the cockpit voice recorder to the families of the victims, so she could hear what had happened. She wanted to know what had gone wrong, why Tom's plan hadn't worked.

Previously, family members of victims of plane crashes had never been allowed to hear the recordings from the cockpit. Deena worked with congressmen and the FBI to bring this change about. "I wanted to hear Tom's voice. I needed his life to count for something," she said.

She was successful. In April 2002, the recordings were released, and Deena and the family members of the other passengers finally learned what had happened to bring that plane down. "Through my leadership role, I discovered that one person can make a difference," she said.

That was all it took. Suddenly, Deena found her life moving in a different direction. When Anna Clare started preschool, Deena went to work as a speaker for the Young America's Foundation, an organization dedicated to educating students about conservative principles. Then she volunteered for the 20th Century Club, which provides housing at no cost to cancer patients. On the first anniversary of Tom's death, Deena launched the Tom Burnett Family Foundation. A year later, the foundation introduced a new social studies program designed to teach students responsibility, accountability, patriotism, and service.

"Being a good citizen was so important to Tom," Deena explained. "This program teaches students how to be good citizens. Tom's niece, Kathleen West, and her friend wrote it for eighth-graders, but Brownies, Girl Scouts, Boy Scouts, and boarding schools also utilize the program. It is a great way to honor him."

In June 2002, Deena moved to Little Rock, Arkansas. When she told her parents she was moving, they relocated to Little Rock, as well. Her brother, Scotty, and her stepsister, Kristen, soon moved within driving distance.

"The wagons circled around me," Deena said. "I wasn't recognized as much in Little Rock, so the media left me alone. I was able to choose which interviews I wanted to do. My family was so supportive, and they got me through every day."

Halley, Madison, and Anna Clare each handled their father's death differently. "Halley kept it inside," Deena said. "She didn't talk about it, but sometimes I'd look over at her, and tears would be streaming down her face. She'd wipe them away when she noticed I was looking at her. Madison wanted to talk about it constantly. She told everyone that her dad had died. Anna Clare became very angry and short-tempered. She cried a lot."

Before long, Deena was approached about writing a book. She thought about it and decided she wanted to write it for her children. She was afraid that with so much media attention on more than three thousand people who had lost their lives that day, their father would get lost, and she wanted to chronicle his life and heroism for them. She began telling her story to Anthony F. Giombetti, her co-author for *Fighting Back: Living Life Beyond Ourselves*.

"I didn't intend for it to get published, but I'm really proud of it now," she said. "It took five years to write it, and I cried a lot during that time, but it also kept me sane. Anthony became a very good friend."

During the first five years after Tom's death, Deena attended numerous memorials for Tom and other victims of 9/11. She threw herself into volunteerism, at one time serving on the boards of nine different charities. She volunteered at school and church. And she discovered she had a knack for fundraising.

She also found love again. Deena had not dated anyone since Tom died, and she was hesitant about meeting the man a friend had suggested she meet. Finally, she said he could call her. Rodney Bailey called Deena, and they began talking every day over the next month. She told him that her husband had passed away, but she didn't mention Tom's name.

Finally, Deena agreed to meet Rodney for lunch at a restaurant, and she told him about her husband. Big tears welled in Rodney's eyes as she spoke. He looked at her, and said, "Your husband was a hero." Deena was touched by his respect for Tom.

Deena and Rodney dated for two and a half years and were married in June 2006. Rodney had a son, Tanner, and through the marriage, Deena's daughters got a new big brother they adored.

"Rodney's a big guy, a teddy bear. He has a very strong faith, strong family ties, and he's very patriotic. He's quiet and easygoing, very laid back. I became Tom in the relationship," she said, laughing. "He has a big heart and has never minded the devotion the girls and I have for Tom."

For the next few years, Deena dedicated herself to her family and her volunteer work. By the tenth anniversary of 9/11, she was exhausted. She had been reliving Tom's death every day for months through attending memorials and ceremonies. She was also fundraising for a variety of charities. It was a difficult time for her, and she decided she needed to regroup. "I knew I had to do something different, but I didn't know what I wanted to do," she said.

In 2012, Deena was approached with an opportunity for direct selling that allows women to own their own skincare businesses. Founded by the creators of Proactive skincare products, Rodan + Fields is dedicated to "changing skin and lives" across America through its partnership with buildOn, a movement whose mission is to teach impoverished urban youth how to rebuild their communities through service.

Deena embraced this new opportunity, and she now teaches women how to start their own businesses. "This is about empowering women to change their own lives while helping others," she said. "They then give back a portion of the money they make to the charity of their choice. One lady in Seattle gives 100 percent of her profit to an organization that helps cancer patients. Another woman was an orphan, so she gives all of the money she makes to an organization that tutors children and provides scholarships. Women all over the country are making enormous paychecks and giving back to their communities. It's a beautiful thing."

Deena's life is a happy one. She has a wonderful marriage with Rodney. Tanner is twenty-six years old, Halley and Madison are now twenty, and Anna Clare is eighteen. Deena and her girls have survived the worst tragedy in American history with strength and grace.

"I've told Tom's story a thousand times, and I still cry every time I tell it," Deena said. "It seems fitting somehow that our last conversation was over a telephone because so much of our marriage was spent that way. My girls and I are so proud of the person that Tom was, and we will continue to celebrate his life for the rest of ours."

For more information, please visit www.tomburnettfoundation.org, www.hopeawayfromhome.org, www.buildon.org, www.yaf.org, and www.rodanandfields.com.

STANLEY ROBERTS

Banned NBA star rebounds to help kids

"The ground was so far below him, he could barely make it out through the grey mists that whirled around him, but he could feel how fast he was falling, and he knew what was waiting for him down there. Even in dreams, you could not fall forever. He would wake up in the instant before he hit the ground, he knew. You always woke in the instant before you hit the ground."

—George R. R. Martin, author

O n November 24, 1999, Head Coach Larry Brown of the Philadelphia 76ers called Stanley Roberts and asked him to come to a meeting before practice. Stanley had recently signed with the 76ers, and he and Larry shared a special bond. Larry had faith in the seven-foot center, nicknamed "Franchise," who had been league-hopping and battling injuries for years.

Stanley had planned to sit out a season, to regroup and straighten out his life, but as it always had, basketball led the way, and he followed along.

Stanley flew to Philadelphia for an interview, signed a contract, and was right back in the game. Just before the last preseason game, he returned to Houston to get some of his things.

When he walked into Larry's office a few days later, Stanley was in a great mood. His youngest daughter and her mother were flying in to see the game, and he was excited that they would be there to watch him play.

Larry wasn't alone. He had a pained look on his face as he introduced Stanley to a disciplinary officer from the National Basketball Association (NBA). Stanley listened intently as the man read aloud from a piece of paper he was holding.

Stunned, Stanley tried to comprehend the words he was hearing.

He walked out of Larry's office and went to the locker room. He stared at the jersey with number fifty-three emblazoned on it, swallowing back the tears that threatened.

Everyone in the locker room had already heard. ESPN had announced the breaking news.

Under the new anti-drug rules, Stanley Roberts had just become the first basketball player in the history of the league to be banned from the NBA indefinitely.

S tanley Roberts didn't have any great ambition to play basketball when he was young. His brother played, and his uncles played, but Stanley simply wasn't interested. He was more of a mama's boy and preferred staying close to home.

He grew up in Hopkins, South Carolina, in a singlewide trailer that housed his father, Robert; his mother, Isabella; his older brother, Wayne; and his younger sister, Judith. They were a tight-knit family and followed a simple routine—school, home, chores, baths, bed. On Sundays, they attended church. Isabella, a very spiritual woman, made sure of that.

Although the family was poor, Stanley didn't really notice. He was just like everyone else in his neighborhood, except that he was much taller than other children his age. By the time he reached eighth grade, he stood six feet ten inches tall.

His brother, Wayne, was a senior at Lower Richland High School, where he played basketball on the varsity team. Before Wayne graduated, he asked his coach to watch out for Stanley, who would be attending the school the next year.

"Does he play basketball?" Coach Jim Childers asked Wayne.

"No, but he's six-foot-ten," Wayne responded.

The coach showed up at Stanley's junior high school to recruit him soon after. "I was literally horrible," Stanley said. "I didn't know anything about basketball."

Coach Childers, impressed with Stanley's size, sent him to a camp run by former basketball stars Alex English and Ralph Sampson. "I wasn't in good physical shape," Stanley said, "and about a minute into my first workout, I was exhausted. I stayed there for a week, but I didn't like it. My brother asked me what I thought about it, and I said it sucked."

Wayne recruited Stanley's uncles to teach him the game.

"They took me to a nearby elementary school and beat me up for a month and a half," Stanley recalled. "They whipped me into shape and taught me the basic rules."

Excited by the teenager's potential, Coach Childers sent Stanley to a team camp. "There, I learned how to rebound and ended up being named most valuable player of the camp," Stanley said. "I remember coming home still thinking I sucked."

When one of the trainers told Stanley that the coach wanted him to practice with the varsity team, Stanley thought, *not again*. The conditioning was rough, but he made it through.

In his sophomore year, his basketball IQ was still not very high, but he played on the varsity team and was named Third Team All-American by the end of the season. "I ended up being pretty good. We made it to the semifinals in my sophomore year, and then in my junior and senior years, we won the state championship."

As a high school player, Stanley developed a love/hate relationship with basketball. He liked playing in the actual games, but he hated the conditioning required to be on the court. He played basketball because he was tall and because that was what the men in his family did.

Although he didn't have the same passion for the game that others in his family had, when the college scholarship offers started rolling in, Stanley thought, *okay, I'll go to college, and I'll play basketball.*

Universities from all over the country began recruiting efforts. By his junior year, Stanley had narrowed his choices to three colleges—Louisiana State University (LSU), University of South Carolina (USC), and Georgia Tech (GT). He wasn't sure which college to choose, but a family tragedy helped him with the decision.

In April 1997, Stanley's brother killed an eighteen-year-old boy in self-defense and wounded two other boys. The family feared that Wayne would spend the rest of his life in prison, but a USC coach hinted to Isabella that if Stanley signed with USC, he would make sure Wayne did not go to prison.

Stanley began to feel the pressure. His brother was facing life in prison, and it was now up to him to prevent that. This didn't sit well with Isabella, who told Stanley not to make a decision until the trial was over. "Wayne was in the wrong place at the wrong time and was later acquitted of all charges," Stanley said.

During that time, Stanley became impressed with LSU's coach, Dale Brown. "Coach Brown called every other night to check on me," he said. "He showed an interest in my life. He said, 'I'm not recruiting you as a basketball player, I'm recruiting you as a human being.' He was a man of his word."

The now seven-foot-tall Stanley enrolled in LSU and moved to Louisiana to begin his college career. He was not allowed to play his freshman year because he was academically ineligible. His sophomore year, however, sealed his future as a professional basketball player. Stanley, Chris Jackson, and freshman Shaquille O'Neal gave LSU an incredibly talented team for one season, arguably the best in LSU's history. Shaq went on to superstardom, in part because of the competition Stanley provided him. When those two mastodons went up against each other in practice, everyone stopped what they were doing to watch. Shaq has publicly admitted that Stanley was the better player back then. "Yeah, I worked him out pretty good at LSU," Stanley said, laughing.

The Tigers ended up losing in the second round of the 1990 NCAA tournament

Laura and George W. Bush visit with Tonja Myles at the White House.

Dr. Bobby Smith shares his message of hope with fellow police officers.

Kristen Maddox talks with guest speaker Stephen Baldwin
at the 2015 annual Power of Hope event.

Bea Aikens promotes Problem Gambling Awareness Month
with advocates at the Foundation for Recovery.

From left, YASNY Entertainment's Daniel Balsz, Hollywood film actor Danny Trejo, Digital Spatula's Steve Taylor, and YASNY Entertainment's Tracy Balsz spend time together on the set of *Rock Bottom and Back*.

From left, Kirk LaGrange, social media director for Mission Media; Earl B. Heard, coauthor of *Rock Bottom and Back;* Devin Black, cameraman and editor for Mission Media; Stanley Roberts, former NBA star; and Steven Scaffidi, producer/director for Mission Media, visit during a filming session for the *Rock Bottom and Back* DVD.

Father and son Jerry and Whitney Strickland at The Wheelhouse

Whitney Strickland (center) shares his knowledge of racecars with children
in the Galveston Urban Ministries after-school program.

Maurice "Termite" Watkins as a young boxer

Maurice "Termite" Watkins (back row, center) with
the Iraqi boxing team he trained for the Olympics

American hero Tom Burnett, who lost his life on United Flight 93
after storming the cockpit on 9/11

Theresa Westbrook comforts an attendee at the In His Presence
conference in Denton, Texas.

Stanley Roberts shines on the court at LSU.

Donna and Billy Rivers

Susan Mustafa and Earl B. Heard, coauthors of *Rock Bottom and Back*

George Mills shares insight on human trafficking at the
2016 Trafficking Hope Gala. (Photograph courtesy of Jenn Oken)

after a 23-9 season. The Associated Press awarded Stanley Third-Team All-SEC honors because of the 14.1 points per game, sixty blocked shots, and 9.8 rebounds per game he accumulated that season.

Shaq, however, was more motivated and a better student. When Stanley failed one class he needed to maintain a 2.0 grade point average, he became ineligible to play. "It was Dairy Science," Stanley said. "I called Coach Brown, and he offered to let me live with him while I got my grades up. In my mind, I knew I wasn't going to pass that class, so I decided to quit school and move to the pros instead."

The problem was that Stanley made his decision too late to make the NBA draft that season.

He called Coach Childers, who recommended an agent in Baton Rouge, Oscar Shoenfelt. Stanley signed with him the following day. Oscar fronted him $20,000, and Stanley bought a used SUV.

"Oscar was new to the business, and he took a chance with me. I took a chance with him, as well. The next day, an overseas team, Real Madrid, was about to sign a player from Dallas when they saw my name come across the wire. That night, we hashed out a deal," Stanley said.

At nineteen years old, the giant teenager from South Carolina signed a million dollar deal to play basketball in Spain. "I didn't want to go to Spain. I wanted to party," he remembered.

The day before he was scheduled to leave, Stanley bought a case of beer, called some friends, and went to the Greek Theatre at LSU to do just that. Afterwards, while giving a teammate a ride home in his SUV, an insect flew in the window and bit Stanley on the back of his hand. He didn't think anything of it. He dropped his friend off and headed to IHOP to meet his girlfriend.

"What's wrong?" she said when he sat down at the table where she was waiting.

"Nothing," Stanley said.

"Your face is swollen," she said.

Stanley went to the bathroom and looked in the mirror. His face was almost unrecognizable. He rushed back to his girlfriend. "Get me to the hospital fast," he said.

At the hospital, he lost consciousness while nurses were taking his blood pressure. When he awoke, he saw himself sitting in a wheelchair and someone was saying, "Code Blue."

"I was brought to a small room with swinging doors, and I could see fear in the eyes of everyone around me. It was like I was out of my body watching them,"

Stanley said.

The doctors gave him three shots in his right arm, but he didn't respond. So they tried one in his left arm. Nothing happened. The doctor asked the nurse for an EpiPen. That worked. When Stanley awoke, a nurse told him he had flatlined.

Stanley described for the doctor what he had watched in his out-of-body state. The doctor informed him incredulously that everything he described had happened.

A few days later, Stanley flew to Spain. When he got there, he failed his physical, due to carbon monoxide poisoning caused by emissions from the vehicle he had bought. Something was telling him that maybe Spain wasn't a good idea.

Stanley spent the next month in a hotel room surrounded by humidifiers. The doctors gave him steroids, which caused him to gain weight. "By the time I recovered, the media was talking about me like a dog," he said. "Real Madrid had paid a million bucks for an overweight American."

Stanley was prescribed fluid pills and diet pills to lose weight. The problem was that the instructions were written in Spanish. He accidentally took three fluid pills and one diet pill each day, instead of vice versa. "The weight flew off, and I was able to play a few games," he said. "During the tenth game of the season, I walked to the huddle and passed out from dehydration."

By the end of the season, Stanley, who loved to have a good time, had begun dabbling in drugs. Young and impulsive, he could not envision the magnitude of that decision. His recklessness caused him to be banned from Spain for three years.

Stanley didn't mind. He was ready to come home.

Back in the States, the Orlando Magic drafted him in the first round. Everyone knew he had the potential to be one of the best centers to ever play the game.

In his first season, Stanley lit up the court and earned NBA All-Rookie Second Team. The next season, the Magic drafted Shaq and traded Stanley, who had hosted Shaq when he came to Orlando. Stanley was traded first to the New York Knicks and then to the Los Angeles Clippers in the first three-way trade of its kind.

Stanley moved to California. In his first season with the Clippers, he averaged 11.3 points per game, with one hundred forty-one blocked shots and 6.2 rebounds per game. He enjoyed the money he made and the celebrity that comes with being an athlete in the NBA. A warm, friendly smile always creased his face, and he made many friends who were willing to party with him during the off-season. If his friends needed money, Stanley was happy to dole it out—thousands at a time. He didn't know how to say no to anyone. And when the cocaine flowed, Stanley was right there saying yes again.

Inside, though, he began to feel an emptiness. Although friends and fans were always around, he began to feel very alone.

Stanley ruptured both of his Achilles tendons and was forced to the sidelines for most of the next two seasons. At that time, he had so many friends living in his home in Los Angeles that he moved into an apartment to get some privacy. He just couldn't ask his friends to leave when they needed a place to live. Stanley was much too nice for that. His generosity was becoming legendary, and he made more and more friends.

He came back to play respectably for two more seasons with the Clippers. "When you're young, you think you're invincible," he said. "I was in so much pain, I couldn't walk after games. I'd take a Vicodin before a game, one during the game, and two after. I couldn't practice. I just played." Doctors eventually discovered that bone spurs were rubbing against his Achilles tendons.

The Clippers weren't happy with him. Stanley was the highest-paid player on the team, and they weren't getting their money's worth. Two ruptured disks in his back didn't help matters. As the season progressed, tensions mounted between Stanley and his coach, Bill Fitch. When Stanley walked out on a practice to be with his girlfriend, who was in labor, he was suspended and fined a hefty amount—more than a quarter of a million dollars.

"By this time, I had started using drugs during the regular season, too," Stanley said. "Whenever I felt down or stressed, I'd use. As my injuries got worse, I used more and more."

Stanley was plagued by a series of injuries for the rest of his career. When the season was over, he finally had the back surgery he needed, but his tenure with the Clippers was over. He was traded to Minnesota and then released after one season.

Soon Stanley signed with a team in Greece, but played only two weeks there before returning home due to another back injury. The Houston Rockets picked him up, allowing Stanley to rehab during the regular season. He was activated for the playoffs and promptly dislocated his shoulder in his first practice. "I had a torn rotator cuff," he said. "That was rough. I tried to play, but couldn't."

The Rockets released him. Stanley's drug use had escalated over the years, and he knew it was time to re-evaluate what he wanted to do with his life. He decided to sit out for a year. Then Larry Brown called, and in 1999, Stanley was banned from the NBA.

"I had to tell my daughter. That was so hard," he said.

Stanley spent the next few weeks with his family, trying to figure out what to do. He was tired, mentally and physically, and hurting.

Then his agent called. A team in Turkey wanted to pick him up. The International Basketball Federation (FIBA) assured him that the NBA ban did not extend to foreign countries. Stanley flew to Istanbul and signed a sweet deal—almost a million dollars for four months. The contract went to FIBA and was rejected. Stanley came home again, this time to play with the Harlem Globetrotters. He got sick and was released soon after.

In November 2000, Stanley was arrested in Houston for possession of cocaine; less than a gram had been found in his car. He spent two weeks in jail. When he was released, he signed with San Diego, an American Basketball Association (ABA) team. The team soon folded, and Stanley headed back to Houston for his court date.

"The judge said, 'Entertainers and athletes think they can get away with anything,' before he sentenced me to five years in prison, which was deferred, three hundred forty hours of community service, and he gave me a $10,000 fine," Stanley said. "For the first three and a half years, I did well."

He soon received an invitation to play ball in Japan, but his passport was revoked because he was behind on child support. Stanley had four children—Stanecia, Stanley Jr., Ysabella, and Cahleed with four different women. He had always wanted to get married and had been engaged several times, but he never made it to the altar. He had been ordered to pay one of his ex-girlfriends $5,000 per month in child support, and for many years, he had made his payments on time. Now, he simply couldn't afford that amount, but a judge refused to lower it because he had the potential to make a lot of money.

"I felt like less than a man," he said. "I couldn't take care of my children. I couldn't work. I had no degree, no manual skills. I began to get really depressed. I thought about suicide, but I couldn't do that to my kids."

Finally, in 2002, the NBA lifted the ban. Stanley played one more season in Puerto Rico before a torn hamstring and dislocated kneecap forced his retirement.

He had spent all of his money on women, friends, cars, houses, and partying, and what he had not spent, he had given away. In need of assistance, Stanley consulted a financial advisor he had met through a friend. The man advised him to borrow money against the equity in his house in Orlando and property he owned in South Carolina. "The guy falsified the documents and gave me only ten percent of the loan's value. He stole the rest. I didn't find out for a year," Stanley said.

By then it was too late. The loan company foreclosed, and the athlete who had made $30 million over the course of his career lost everything, including a partially finished home he had started building for his mother.

Stanley couldn't afford to sit around and mope, and he soon got a job at Fiik Investment & Holdings. His whole life had revolved around basketball, but now he had to learn to survive in corporate America. It wasn't an easy transition, but at this point, he was grateful to have an income. He had stayed away from drugs for more than three years, and he had hopes of getting back on top through investment banking.

Then his fiancée broke up with him. "That was it. I was done. I went out that night and partied with some friends."

He failed a drug test the next morning and went to jail for three weeks. "The judge wanted to put me in rehab, but I didn't think I needed it," Stanley said.

When he got out of jail, he lived with his ex-fiancée's mother for a few weeks until his boss loaned him a corporate apartment. One night, Stanley, who had become mired in depression, sat in that apartment staring at the cocaine lined out on the table in front of him. He began crying, begging God to take his addiction away.

The next morning, he was drug tested. "God will answer your prayers," Stanley said. "Maybe not the way you want Him to answer, but He does answer."

The judge sent Stanley to jail without issuing a release date. He spent thirty-two days behind bars before he was sent to mandatory rehab. "It was supposed to be a ninety-day program, but I spent seven months there," Stanley said.

Because of his mother's strong faith, Stanley had always believed in God. He could quote the Bible easily. It had been ingrained into him. The problem was that he wasn't living the words that flowed so easily from his lips. Through a program called "Pathway to Recovery" and a man named Lawrence Robertson, Stanley began to change that.

"Lawrence made me deal with my issues. He made me realize that I had an empty hole in me that I needed to fill. God had spoken to me so many times, but I had ignored Him," Stanley said. "He had my full attention now."

One such instance had happened the year before on a flight from Los Angeles to Houston. The night before the flight, Stanley had gone out partying—getting high, drinking, acting like he was having a good time with his friends—but inside, he felt like he was dying. He returned to his hotel despairing of ever getting well. Feeling suicidal, he had sat in his hotel room, crying. "I told God, 'I'm hitting bottom. If I don't hear from You, I'm done.'"

The next morning, he boarded the plane to find a group of Mormons sitting in first class. Stanley sat in his seat and put on his sunglasses and headphones, hoping no one would bother him. He could feel the woman seated next to him, staring. Finally, she said, "Excuse me. I don't want to bother you, but God told me to tell you it's going to be all right. Keep going. I don't know why I'm telling you this, but you have to keep fighting."

"Again, God answered my prayers in His own way," Stanley said.

After he finished the rehabilitation program, Stanley began attending Central Baptist Church in Katy, Texas. For six weeks, he slipped in quietly, sat in the last pew, listened to the pastor's message, and left. Finally, a man named Randy Ingram approached him and said, "You've been here every Sunday for six weeks. You're a member now." Stanley joined the church.

For the next two years, Stanley drifted from job to job—a Cadillac dealership, a messenger service, a construction site. He began coaching basketball at camps for kids. Through his work with the children, the hole inside him began to fill. By now, Stanley was forty years old and determined to live his life for God. "I prayed that God would send me where He wanted me to be," Stanley said. "He sent me back to school."

One of the best gifts Stanley reaped from his basketball career was a lifelong friendship with Coach Dale Brown. Throughout the years, the coach had called him repeatedly to ask him if he wanted to return to school. This time when Coach Brown called, Stanley pulled out his laptop and went to LSU's website. He filled out the financial aid questionnaire and soon received a letter stating that he had been approved.

Stanley moved to Baton Rouge and began attending LSU. It wasn't easy. He had been diagnosed with dyslexia, and so much had changed in the ensuing years. Everything was computerized now. With the help of the administrative staff, Stanley moved into a small apartment in married housing. He got a student job at the Carl Maddox Field House and worked nights at a campus convenience store. For four and a half years, he lived on a modest budget, studied hard, and hated life. Coach Brown encouraged him every step of the way. "He thinks he's my dad," Stanley said, laughing.

At the beginning of his last semester, Stanley underwent triple bypass surgery. He didn't let that deter him. He took accelerated courses for the credits he needed, and in the fall of 2012, Stanley graduated.

He walked up to the platform to receive his degree in sports administration with a big smile on his face. The audience erupted in applause. As he stood on that stage, his massive frame covered in a long gown, his mother and Coach Brown clapped louder than anyone. This day had been a long time coming.

Recently, Stanley was named an LSU Legend in the 2016 class of Allstate® SEC Basketball Legends. He still resides in Baton Rouge, where he works in staffing and recruiting for Chicago Bridge & Iron Company. He often speaks to teenagers and college students about his life experiences, and he donates his time to coach kids at summer camps. His mission is to help them learn from the mistakes he made. The man who so hated to practice has discovered that he enjoys teaching children the discipline necessary to succeed. In 2015, he served as assistant coach at Ascension Christian High School. He is also involved with Pat's Coats for Kids, a community drive in Baton Rouge that distributes winter coats to children in need.

Although he once experienced an incredible amount of celebrity, now Stanley prefers to stay out of the limelight, giving back to his community, as he says, "on the sly." The gentle giant doesn't like to be credited with the work he does, preferring instead to give the glory to God. "I live a simple life now, and I'm so much happier than I used to be. God has blessed me through people like my mom, Dale Brown, and Lawrence Robertson. I lost everything—fame, fortune, my career—but all of that was never my dream. My dream was the wife, the kids, the white picket fence. Instead, I ended up in basketball and began using drugs. Through the grace of God, I was able to find my way back. My job now is to share His grace with other kids like me."

Even in his worst moments, Stanley always gave to anyone who needed his help, and his generous spirit has reaped him many rewards. Today, he loves nothing more than to watch a child he mentored succeed. He dedicates his life to helping children become the best that they can be.

For more information, please visit www.wbrz.com/pages/pats-coats-for-kids.

DR. MARK LAASER

Pastor's fall shines light on sex addiction and recovery

"I have absolutely no pleasure in the stimulants in which I sometimes so madly indulge. It has not been in the pursuit of pleasure that I have periled life and reputation and reason. It has been the desperate attempt to escape from torturing memories, from a sense of insupportable loneliness and a dread of some strange impending doom."

—Edgar Allan Poe

D r. Mark Laaser, pastor and director of a faith-based medical clinic in Sioux City, Iowa, walked into the board meeting, wondering why his schedule had been cancelled for the day. He knew something important must have happened.

"Sit down," someone said, when he entered the room.

Mark could feel the tension in the air.

He sat down and listened as the members of the board of directors outlined what they knew. With every word, Mark sank farther and farther into his chair, his heart pounding, his face reddening. He wanted to hide under the table.

"Pervert," one member said loudly.

"The clinic is being sued for malpractice," another member said.

"As of this moment, you no longer work here," someone else said.

Mark tried to catch his breath as his past caught up to him right there in front of his colleagues. He tried to speak, but couldn't. He had no defense, no explanation for the things he had done.

Only a physician, who was a recovering alcoholic, displayed any sympathy. "Your sins with sex are no different from mine with alcohol," he said, looking at Mark with kindness in his eyes.

And then came the final blow. A female therapist, who seemed angrier than the rest, said, "You've got to tell your wife. You've got to tell her now," she said. "Let's go. I'll follow you home."

Mark's heart plummeted into his stomach. Life, as he had known it, was over.

M ark looked around to make sure no one was watching, then he shoved the *Playboy* magazine inside his jacket and hurried out of the drugstore. He was eleven years old, and like many other boys his age, he was fascinated by nudity. Hurrying back to the parsonage, he hid the magazine in his room, his heart racing in anticipation of what he would soon find between those pages. He knew what he was doing was wrong, but that made it more exciting.

Mark's father, Robert, was a pastor and a World War II veteran. Robert, definitely the man of the house, had a large personality, and his family loved and respected him. Mark's mother, Juanita, a nurse, cared for her family and her patients with equal fervor. The family lived near St. Louis, Missouri, where Mark and his younger brother, David, shared a happy home life. The parsonage was usually filled with other pastors and members of Robert's congregation who came to him for advice and prayer requests. The pastor always made time for those who needed his help, and he loved serving the Lord. In his home, Robert made sure his children were nurtured with daily Bible readings and prayer.

Robert had been sexually abused as a child, and unfortunately, this type of abuse can become a cycle that is perpetrated from generation to generation. When he began visiting Mark's bedroom at night, the young boy had no comprehension about what was being done to him or how that abuse would later manifest. It was simply part of their routine, like having dinner or watching television.

"It wasn't heinous or awful," Mark said. "It wasn't frightening. It was just a normal part of daily life. I was three years old when it began, and I had no ability to process what was happening."

The abuse lasted for several months and then stopped.

From the time Mark was about five years old, he had urges he didn't understand. He had no concept of sex, but he was fascinated with female bodies and often thought about what women would look like if they were naked.

Because he had been too young to fully comprehend what had been done to him, Mark grew up admiring and respecting his father, witnessing firsthand the many lives that were improved through Robert's ministry. Mark tried hard to make Robert proud, and as he got older, he did not go through a rebellious phase like some teenagers do.

He did, however, become obsessed with pornography. Each month, he went to a local drugstore and stole a magazine. He kept his collection in his garage and became quite popular with other boys his age when they discovered he had accumulated a lending library. Although he felt guilty, he couldn't stop himself.

"When I was twelve, I went to a church camp," Mark recalled. "I prayed that God would help me stop what I was doing, and I wrote '*Playboy* magazine' on a note and threw it into the bonfire. When my desire for pornography didn't stop, I was disappointed that God didn't answer my prayer, but back then I expected Him to do all the work."

As a teenager, Mark began dating, and he always behaved like a good Christian boy. He was respectful, but needy. "Several of my early girlfriends felt a lot of sexual energy from me, but I never pushed too far," he said.

Instead, he immersed himself in his magazines and self-gratification. While it is normal for teenage boys to indulge in this activity, Mark was far beyond the norm. Obsessed with pornography, he lived in a fantasy world.

At the age of sixteen, Mark attended another Christian camp and accepted Jesus as his Savior. Again, he asked the Lord to take away his obsession with porn. Again, God didn't answer his prayer.

When he was a senior in high school, Mark met a beautiful girl named Debbie. "We fell in love in an infatuated sort of way," he said. "As our relationship progressed, we made out, but we didn't cross any lines. I had been taught to be respectful of the women I dated." The relationship continued even when Debbie moved three hours away to attend college.

Although Mark had ambitions to be a professional tennis player, his talent didn't match his love of the game, so he decided to follow in his father's footsteps. He attended Princeton Theological Seminary, where he delved into biblical philosophies and developed the skills necessary to become a pastor. "I wanted to be like my father," Mark said. "I admired the work that he did."

While in college, Mark sometimes thought about asking one of his professors for guidance. Throughout his life, he had hidden his sexual addiction from everyone, and he desperately wanted someone to help him to stop. He was fearful, however, that he would be excluded from the ministry, so he didn't seek help. He could feel the weight of shame and guilt, but as with any addict, his "drug" offered only temporary relief. He sought that relief more and more often.

Three years into college, Mark and Debbie became engaged, and in 1972, they were married. "On our honeymoon, we had sex for the first time," Mark said. "We were both virgins. I hoped that my addiction would go away when I got married, but that didn't happen. I began to feel resentful that my marriage had not solved my problem. We had a normal sex life, but if Debbie was tired and said no, I didn't see that as legitimate. I thought I was entitled, and I became angry."

That anger enabled Mark to cross his moral convictions. He was angry with God, angry with himself, and angry with Debbie, but his wife had no idea. As the years went by, she sensed that something was wrong in her marriage, but she didn't know what. At times, Mark was distant, but he always assured her that everything was okay.

Mark went on to earn his Ph.D. from the University of Iowa in pastoral counseling and soon began his career, sometimes treating clients who suffered from his own affliction. In 1976, Mark and Debbie had their first child, Sarah. Debbie embraced motherhood and hoped that the new baby would help bring her and Mark closer than ever. She was unaware that her husband was about to cross another line.

Mark's addiction began escalating to the point that he had a sexual encounter outside of his marriage. "It didn't involve intercourse, and as soon as it was over, I got scared. I loved Debbie. She was a wonderful wife. I vowed I would never do that again."

Mark didn't confess to Debbie, and soon he felt a strong urge to repeat his behavior. He decided that a massage parlor wouldn't be as serious an offense, that it wouldn't really be cheating. "The woman there was an old classmate, and it was embarrassing, but that didn't stop us," he said.

Over the next few years, Mark convinced himself that as long as he didn't have intercourse with another woman, he was still being faithful to his wife. The obsession with porn and self-gratification continued, and as new technologies emerged, other avenues for release became available. He progressed to videos, R-rated movies, and then cable television. "I made sure we had all the right channels," he said. "I would wait until Debbie went to sleep at night and then sneak downstairs to watch porn. Even with all of my training and the pastors in my life, I couldn't be honest with Debbie, with anyone. I became a pretty good liar."

At the clinic, clients often related similar problems. When one guilt-ridden client, in particular, shared that he had cheated on his wife, Mark counseled him with the usual Christian-based platitudes, as he had been taught to do. The young man looked down, his guilt weighing heavily on him.

Mark stared at him for a moment, realizing that he was looking in a mirror. Shame flowed through him as an image of the masseuse from the day before flashed through his mind, and then a picture of his wife, so pretty, sweet, and loving.

"Pray that God will give you strength to resist temptation," he said, standing up to usher the young man out.

"It was the blind leading the blind," Mark said. "I had no idea of the process that was necessary to heal this sort of addiction. Back then no one discussed sexual addiction. It wasn't a recognized diagnosis, and I couldn't help him because I didn't have a clue how to help myself."

Before long, Debbie and Mark had two more children, Jon and Ben. Debbie still sensed something was wrong in her marriage, and at times, she felt a bit lonely. She tried to reach Mark, but there was always an invisible barrier that she didn't understand. He said the right things—that he loved her, that she was pretty—and they made love regularly, but she knew something was missing.

Mark began having encounters with more women and continued visiting massage parlors occasionally. "I was so full of shame and guilt, which is part of the cycle," he said. "You medicate by doing it again and again."

By 1987, Mark was medicating regularly.

He worked as the director of a faith-based medical clinic that incorporated pastoral counseling with holistic health. He spent his weekends pastoring at a church in Sioux City, and he occasionally taught at Morningside College. He also served as a member of the school board. At the clinic, he worked long hours as a marriage and family counselor. "By this time, I was out of control," he said. "I just got deeper and deeper. I knew if I confessed, I could get divorced and lose my job. I couldn't take that chance. I was drowning."

Then one of his clients, a woman with whom he had shared a sexual encounter, reported him, and Mark's worst fears were realized. On March 17, 1987, he walked into that boardroom and was called a pervert by an angry therapist. The therapist followed Mark to his home. Mark was fearful of what would happen next. Having just lost his job, he knew he was in danger of losing his family.

The therapist marched into their home and instructed Debbie that she needed to get a babysitter, then waited while arrangements were made. When the children were gone, she told Debbie what her husband had done, using language similar to what she had used in the board meeting.

Debbie was shocked. She and Mark had been married fifteen years, and she had always trusted him implicitly. She didn't know what to say, what to do. She sat there, stunned, as her world shattered.

"I had so many emotions—anger, sorrow, but this explained so much of the loneliness I had felt in my marriage," Debbie would later reveal.

When the woman left, Mark sat in his favorite chair in abject despair. He couldn't look at his wife. He couldn't say anything. What could he say? He had been caught red-handed, and it was time to pay the piper.

"Debbie showed me the face of grace that day," he said. "She walked over to my chair, and she said, 'We're going to get through this. We'll survive.'"

Survival was not easy. The story of the marriage counselor and pastor who had violated his moral and ethical obligations hit the news. Soon the story was everywhere, and there was nowhere to hide. Mark resigned his position as pastor of his church. "I couldn't face them," he said. "I just couldn't." He also resigned from the college where he taught and from the school board. His terrible addiction to sex had cost him everything.

Because of the sensational news coverage, Debbie and Mark had to explain to their children that Daddy had broken promises to Mommy and had been unfaithful. "We're going to get through this together. You don't have to worry about a divorce," they reassured the children.

At first, Debbie wasn't so sure. She had been blindsided, and her reactions in the beginning were purely instinctual. She was in shock and getting by one day at a time, one hour at a time. She had children, three beautiful children, and a husband that she deeply loved. Suddenly, her life had become fodder for the media, and all that she once thought was real and good had become a nightmare. Mixed in there, though, was a sense of relief. She now had an explanation for the emptiness she had felt in her marriage.

Reeling, Mark didn't know what to do. Then he experienced another face of grace. Dr. David Paulrud, the recovering alcoholic who had extended him sympathy at the board meeting, suggested that Mark go to a treatment center in Minneapolis, Minnesota. Dr. Paulrud sat next to him when Mark made the call and went with him to the airport.

"It was good that I had so many consequences," Mark said. "I had no choice but to take this seriously."

Although his life was falling apart around him, Mark, too, felt relief. He didn't have to hide any more. He no longer had to lie. Finally, he would have a chance to live the godly life he had always wanted to live but had been unable to achieve for reasons he did not yet understand.

At the treatment facility, Mark began learning how to take ownership of his addiction and how to recover. After he had been there two weeks, the facility hosted a family week, and Debbie flew to Minneapolis to participate. She jumped in with both feet, determined to learn everything she could about her husband's addiction. It wasn't easy. She had some codependency issues of her own to conquer, and at times, she felt very alone. She had to learn how to control her anger, how to forgive, and how to regain her trust in the man who had repeatedly violated their vows.

"In treatment, I admitted everything to Debbie," Mark said. "She chose to look at my behavior as an addiction, and she got a lot of help early on about how to avoid blaming herself. It was never her fault. She is the love of my life. The problem was me."

Upon his release, Mark returned to Sioux City, where he was referred to a counseling center. For the next year, he went through individual, group, and marital counseling. He was determined to get well, to make things right for Debbie and his children. "I was committed to being sexually sober and the man God wanted me to be," he said.

Six months into counseling, a therapist suggested that Mark return to Kansas, to the parsonage where he had lived when his father had abused him. Mark went to Wichita, and that night, visual memories resurfaced, memories that explained his lifelong obsession with sex. While it was difficult to reconcile those memories with the man he had so admired, Mark, recognizing that this is a generational sickness, eventually forgave his father.

"Remembering what had happened helped define who I am today," he said. "It made me more empathetic and helped me understand abuse."

With the help of numerous therapists, his wife, and others he encountered along the way, Mark began to rebuild his life. He and Debbie moved their family to Minneapolis, where they could be anonymous once again. The facility where Mark had received his initial treatment soon hired him as the director of alumni relations. When Dr. Patrick Carnes, founder and director of the treatment center, realized that Mark had a Ph.D. and clerical training, he began training him to work with sexual addicts. In addition to his marketing responsibilities, Mark soon began teaching and training others.

In 1988, Dr. Carnes received an invitation to speak at a Christian counselor conference, but he felt that Mark would be a better fit. He suggested Mark take his place. Mark was leery and wondered if he should tell his story at the conference. He decided that the best way to illustrate the seriousness of sexual addiction was through his personal experience. He took a deep breath and plunged in.

Mark didn't know that an acquisitions editor for Zondervan was in the audience. When he finished speaking, she approached him and said, "If you can put into a book what you said today, we'll publish it."

Mark went home and wrote a proposal, then submitted it to the editor, but he didn't hear back from her. Months later, he learned that she had passed away. Out of the blue one day, her successor called and said, "Why don't we have your book? We want it."

In May 1992, Mark's first book, *Healing the Wounds of Sexual Addiction*, was published. Soon after, Debbie penned her side of the story and published a book, *Shattered Vows: Hope and Healing for Women Who Have Been Sexually Betrayed.* "That opened the door for so many wonderful things," Mark said.

Since that time, he has authored or coauthored fifteen books, including two with Debbie and his latest, *The Fight of Your Life: Manning Up to the Challenge of Sexual Integrity*, with Dr. Tim Clinton.

Mark worked at the treatment center for four years, and then, for the next ten years, he worked with hospitals to establish treatment programs for sexual addiction. He became a pioneer in the field and began speaking about the subject nationally and internationally. "I had so many people asking me why I didn't do counseling, but I had bad counselor shame," he said.

People kept asking. Finally, with almost fifteen years between him and his addiction, Mark and Debbie, who is also a licensed marriage and family therapist, decided to take a risk. In 2005, they opened Faithful & True, a ministry and counseling center, where they focused solely on treating sexual addiction. "Men come to us from all over the world," Mark said. And while he recognizes that there are many female sex addicts, Mark concentrates mostly on men. "I'm a recovering male sex addict," he said. "I don't counsel women alone."

It has now been twenty-nine years since Mark walked into that board meeting. He and Debbie resolved their problems long ago and have a strong, loving marriage. Mark has worked hard to earn back the trust and respect of those in the medical profession and those in the clergy. He continues to write and speak, and he hosts a radio podcast called "The Men of Valor Program," which is available on iTunes and on the Faithful & True website. He and Debbie are still dedicated to helping others through the very thing that once tore their lives apart. Through Faithful & True, the couple has facilitated the recovery of numerous addicts, enabling them to live happy and sexually healthy lives.

For Mark, one of the most difficult parts of his journey was his fall from grace inside his denomination. He loved being a pastor and being a vital part of the Christian community. Recently, he was reordained with the former Baptist General Conference, and he feels like he has come full circle. "There are times we are so lost in our darkness that God needs to blow it up to get our attention. He certainly got mine, and since that time, He has poured amazing grace on my life through extraordinary people, like my wife, Dr. Paulrud, the people at the treatment center, the editor from Zondervan."

Mark says the problem of sexual addiction is getting worse because of easy access to pornography on the Internet. "The greatest enemy of sexual health is silence," he said. "My best advice to addicts is this: Break your silence. Help is available. You don't have to deal with your addiction alone. There is hope."

For more information, please visit www.faithfulandtrue.com.

BEA AIKENS

Through loss, former gambler learns to win at life

Bea Aikens walked into her sister's hospital room in Harrisburg, Pennsylvania, clutching a bag filled with prescription bottles. She stared at Lanie for a moment, her heart breaking all over again when she noticed her sister was still unresponsive. She touched Lanie's hand before turning to the intern to give him the bag.

"I found her medication, but I discovered something else," Bea said. "I'm a gambler in recovery. I thought she was in recovery, too. I discovered today that she's been gambling again. I know that gamblers have the highest suicide rate among all addicts. This may have been intentional."

The intern straightened up, listening intently, his eyes brightening at her words. "Did she win?" he asked.

Bea stood there, frozen. It felt like he had just hit her. Her beloved sister, her best friend, was in a medically induced coma with a machine pumping air into her lungs, breathing for her, and this idiot wanted to know if she had won.

Bea wanted to scream, to curse, to punch him, anything to make him understand. *No, she didn't win. She's in a coma.*

Lanie was older than Bea by two and a half years, and she was a rebel. As children growing up in Lemoyne, Pennsylvania, Bea and Lanie had experienced their fair share of spats. Bea was slender, popular in school, a good student. Lanie was overweight, socially awkward, and hated school. Early on, Bea assumed the role of peacemaker in their home, always striving to keep things as harmonious as possible. Their father, Jim Twigg, was a successful real estate broker, and he favored Bea. Lanie knew it. Everyone knew it, but he had his reasons.

Lanie could be stubborn and difficult. She did not want to go to school, and every morning began with the drama of getting Lanie out of bed. Their mother, Betty, would walk into her room, saying, "Good morning, Sunshine. It's a beautiful day." Lanie would groan and roll over, placing her pillow over her head, arguing that she didn't want to go to school until her father came in, yelling, "Lanie, get out of that bed, or I'm going to get you out of it."

Bea, on the other hand, got up early, told everyone "Good morning" in her bright, cheery voice, and got dressed ahead of schedule. She always went the extra mile to gain her parents' approval. As a child, Bea was already learning to wear the mask she would wear for most of her life. "I was the harmony," she said. "That was my personality. I loved Lanie, but we were as different as night and day. I always tried to smooth everything over, but our relationship was somewhat dysfunctional."

Betty was the typical sixties mom—Avon lady, Girl Scout leader, brownie maker. Bea's friends often called her mother "Betty Boop," a nickname that would stay with her for the rest of her life. "My mom was pure love," Bea said. "She was awesome."

Jim was without a doubt the man of the house. He made the rules, and he enforced them, but Bea's was a relatively happy childhood. Jim and Betty loved to socialize, and their home was always filled with friends and business colleagues. Two bars, one downstairs and one upstairs, made serving cocktails convenient, and Bea often spent her evenings preparing drinks for her parents' guests.

Gambling, too, was a part of the social norm in their family. Lottery tickets and scratch-offs were expected stocking stuffers at Christmastime, and Bea's parents would often take off for weekend junkets at nearby casinos. Bea was just seven years old when she won her first bet.

"You always remember your first win," she said. "Mine happened at the Firemen's Festival. They had this giant wheel there, and I put one nickel on the number seven. I won seven nickels. It was so exciting."

Back then, there was no stigma attached to gambling. It was glamorous, exciting, and socially acceptable if you had the money. Everyone had heard, of course, of knees being broken by mafia soldiers when debts couldn't be paid, but that was in the underworld, and Bea's family was upper middle class. For them, gambling was entertainment, like drinking.

Bea took her first drink at the age of twelve and promptly blacked out. The next day, she couldn't remember what had happened. Before long, she took another drink. And another. At a very early age, Bea became skilled at hiding things, not because she was ashamed, but because she didn't want to stir things up. That was Lanie's role.

At the age of fifteen, Bea met the love of her life at Negley Park. She was playing touch football with some friends when she first saw him, and her heart skipped a beat. To Bea, Mike Aikens was the handsomest boy she had ever seen, and she soon learned he had a heart of gold. The two became sweethearts, and several years later, Mike asked her to marry him in the same park where they met.

"My father wasn't too fond of him," Bea explained. "From Dad's perspective, Mike was from the wrong side of the tracks. He was a preacher's son, and my father did everything he could to dissuade me from marrying him."

By the time Bea began her college career at Indiana University of Pennsylvania, she was drinking every day and still having blackouts. She joined Delta Zeta during the disco era and made a lot of new friends. After studying hard each day, she partied hard each night. "I was the chug queen of the sorority," she said. "I was a funny, happy drunk, but I rarely remembered anything the next day. People would tell me, 'Oh, my gosh, you were hilarious last night,' and I had no idea what they were talking about."

Bea and Mike decided not to marry and went their separate ways, but she and Lanie became closer than they had ever been, despite their differences. "Lanie didn't go to college. She worked as a millwright, while I was into fashion and learning. I was studying to be a dietitian, and Lanie was hanging out with guys in hardhats," Bea said. "When we were in our early twenties, we finally had a heart-to-heart talk. To her, it had always seemed like my life was easy, while everything was so difficult for her. We came to a deep understanding of each other that day. She became my best friend, and I became her protector, her champion."

After college, Bea, now a full-blown but high-functioning alcoholic, took a job at a hospital where she was exposed to people suffering with kidney failure, heart failure, and a myriad of other life-threatening diseases. She worked there for a few years, but soon realized that this wasn't the career for her. "I'd get attached to the patients, and then they would die. I just couldn't handle that," she said.

Before long, she met and married Bob Goodwin, a man whose personality bore striking similarities to her father. "He was self-assured, attractive, a take-charge kind of guy. I was twenty-four. He was thirty-seven. They say that a person's emotional maturity stops at the age of addiction. I was a twelve-year-old looking for a father figure, and Bob was an alpha male who enjoyed that role."

Bea enjoyed her marriage for a while, but after a few years, she began to resent being treated like a child. Bob, a successful businessman, loved to brag about his accomplishments, his possessions—particularly his assortment of luxury sports cars—to anyone who would listen. At dinners with friends, Bea would lightly tap his leg under the table when he started bragging, but that never worked. Bob would say, "You can tap me all you want, but I'm not going to shut up," in front of everyone, and Bea would want to crawl under that table.

One time, she stood up to him, and he said, "When you make a hundred thousand dollars a year, then you can make decisions." Bea was mortified.

Another time, they were out with business colleagues and their wives, and one of the wives, Carolyn, said she was going shopping for shoes. Bea said, "Oh, I'd love to go." Bob said, "No. You can't. When you make enough money to go shopping, then you can go." Bea was learning the hard way that in her world, money meant power.

So she went to work, determined to become independent. Her new mantra, "Dig deep. Don't quit," served her well. She began selling real estate, and she was always the first one in the office and the last one to leave. By this time, she and Bob had moved to Boulder City, Nevada, some twenty-six miles southeast of Las Vegas, to be near her parents who had moved there years before. Bea was still drinking heavily, but she hid that side of herself from her business associates. She became successful in her own right, brokering high rises in Las Vegas, and she soon became the chairman of a trust company. Bea was proud of herself, and rightly so, but she had secrets, shameful secrets that she hid from everyone.

Bob, Bea, and Bea's parents often frequented local casinos. Bea soon found herself spending more and more time at the casinos, playing blackjack or slots and drinking even more. She began amassing credit card debt and taking out loans to cover her losses, loans she hid from her husband. She was dually addicted and spiraling out of control.

"Gambling isn't about money," she said. "It's about pain. It takes money to fuel it, but there's never any satiety. I was in pain, unhappy in my marriage, tired of everything in my life being about image. I was wearing a happy mask for the outside world, but inside I was falling apart. I felt so much shame and guilt. I had become a liar to hide my addictions."

On April 14, 1989, Bea was sitting at a blackjack table, drinking a cocktail and placing a bet, when suddenly she felt like she was propelled from her stool. "The pit boss asked me if I was okay. I said 'yes,' but I wasn't. I went into the bathroom and started crying. The pit boss came to check on me. I looked at her and said for the first time in my life, 'I think I'm an alcoholic.'"

The next day, Bea went to her first Alcoholics Anonymous meeting, and she hasn't had another drink since.

But Bea had a bigger addiction—gambling.

Before, when Bob or Bea's parents discovered that she'd been running up credit cards to gamble, they chalked it up to her drinking. "Oh, she was drinking," they would say, like that was an acceptable excuse. Now, Bea had no excuse. And when her mother was diagnosed with lung cancer, Bea went off the deep end.

"The cancer spread to her brain, and she was given three months to live," Bea said. "I would go to work in the morning, sit with her each afternoon, and then when she went to sleep, I would head to the casino and gamble all night. I'd get about an hour's sleep and then go to work. This went on for months. It was exhausting. And shameful. I felt such guilt about being at the casino when my mom might need me. I had an inability to cope, and that was my way of escaping my feelings. My shame piled up, along with my debt. When my mom passed away January 3, 1993, I put every bit of shame, pain, and feeling into a slot machine. I couldn't do it fast enough."

Finally realizing she had a serious problem, Bea answered a questionnaire sponsored by Gamblers Anonymous, which stated that if you answer "yes" to seven of the twenty questions, you are an addicted gambler. Bea answered "yes" to all twenty questions. "I looked so normal that the first time I went to see a therapist who specialized in treating addictions someone said, 'You must be the new therapist.' That's the problem. Unlike other types of addictions, there are no outward signs, no slurred speech, no track marks. You can physically see drug or alcohol addiction. Gamblers show up for work, function normally in their homes. There are no telltale signs. It's a mental illness like any other, but it doesn't look like it."

Everything changed for Bea that day. Through therapy and group meetings, she learned to face her feelings, to cope with her losses, and to become a stronger person. "Bob was so supportive of me through my alcohol recovery and my gambling recovery," she said. "I had been exposed as deceitful and as a liar, and he stood by me. In that respect, Bob was an honorable man."

Through it all, Lanie had been there for Bea. Lanie still lived in Pennsylvania, but they talked on the phone often and took sisters' trips regularly. Soon after their mother passed away, Lanie discovered she had Stage 4 lung cancer. Bea was devastated. Lanie was in her early forties, too young to be stricken with what was surely a death sentence.

By this time, Lanie's relationship with their father had deteriorated and was steadily getting worse. "Lanie ran one of his businesses, and my father became convinced that she was stealing. She wasn't, but he couldn't understand that the cancer, the medications she was taking, and the chemo were making her forgetful."

Jim wanted to confront Lanie, but Bea begged him not to do that. "She's sick," Bea said. "She has cancer." Jim agreed he wouldn't say anything, but the next day, Lanie called Bea sobbing. "He thinks I'm stealing," she cried. Bea was furious, and for the first time in her life, she confronted her father. "That was the death of Harmony, the persona I had assumed," she said. "Standing up to him changed me."

When, a short time later, Lanie had to be rushed to the hospital because she developed a blood clot in her leg, Bea got the call from a friend who worked at the hospital. "It's bad. It's really bad," her friend said. Bea went to tell her father, who was in the Cleveland Clinic battling heart disease and not doing well. "Is there anything you want to say to her?" Bea asked him. He requested that she get him a pen and a piece of paper.

"She stole from me. She could have bankrupted me," he wrote.

That was it. Bea was done. She walked out of the clinic and got on a plane to be with Lanie.

At the Holy Spirit Hospital, Lanie's leg was cut open in an effort to remove the blood clot. While she lay in her hospital bed one night, Lanie received a miracle. "She said it felt like there were claws digging into her shoulders," Bea said. "It was like the angels came that night because the next day we learned that she was cancer free. It's very rare for anyone to survive Stage 4 cancer, but it was completely gone and never returned."

Their father passed away soon after.

Bea went back to her life in Boulder City, refocusing on her career and her marriage.

But then one day, Lanie called. "Beatie, I'm so ashamed," she said, crying. "I've lost everything."

Bea could not understand this because their parents had left them a sizable inheritance.

"I lost it all in Atlantic City," Lanie said. "I'm a compulsive gambler."

Bea's heart sank. She knew exactly what that meant.

"Honey, there's help," she said. "Come to Nevada. You can stay with me." Bea knew that Nevada had more resources than Pennsylvania to help her sister.

Lanie moved to nearby Henderson, Nevada, and stayed for two years, taking her recovery seriously and going through the steps with her sponsor.

"That was such a wonderful time," Bea remembered. "We had so much fun, but eventually she missed her children and her slower-paced life in Pennsylvania."

Lanie returned home and took steps to ensure that she would not be tempted to gamble again. She excluded herself from all of the casinos and gambling establishments in Pennsylvania, New Jersey, and Delaware. An addicted gambler can go to the state gambling control board or any casino and sign a request to be put on an exclusion list, which means they will not be allowed inside a casino. Lanie was committed to her recovery and went to every casino she could find in those states and signed the forms. "That took huge courage," Bea said. "It's so hard to admit you are an addict, but Lanie wanted to ensure that she would never gamble again."

Bea missed Lanie, but over the years, they took many trips together, including one to Tahiti. On this trip, Bob joined them. "It was horrible," Bea said. "Our marriage had begun to deteriorate, and that trip only made things worse. When we came back, I told my sponsor, Jan, that I was going to get divorced."

Before that happened, Bob was diagnosed with cancer, and Bea stayed in the marriage to take care of him, and even fell in love again for a while. "Love had many ebbs and flows in our marriage," Bea said. Bob recovered, but the cracks in their marriage had become unresolvable, and the couple divorced in 2008 after twenty-four years of marriage.

Soon after, on May 28, 2008, Bea got a call that would turn her world upside down. It was her Aunt Bea, whom she had been named after. "You'd better get here fast," Aunt Bea said. "Lanie had a stroke. It'll be a miracle if she survives."

A few minutes later, she called back, sounding more hopeful this time. "They've put her in a coma, but things are looking a little better," Aunt Bea said.

Bea rushed to the airport and flew to Pennsylvania. "I sat by her bedside all night, praying," Bea said. "The next day a gaggle of doctors came in pummeling me about her—'How's her home life? Has she been upset about anything, depressed?' I couldn't comprehend what they were getting at. I said, 'It sounds like you think this was intentional.'"

One of the doctors explained to Bea that nobody could have the amount of serotonin in their body that Lanie had unless it was intentional. They thought perhaps Lanie had taken St. John's Wort with her prescribed antidepressants. When taken together, they can cause serotonin syndrome, a malady that causes the body to feel like it's running a marathon while standing still. The heart races, organ activity speeds up, and in the most severe cases, death is the result. Lanie's diagnosis was serotonin syndrome. The only question was—intentional or accidental? If it wasn't an innocent mixing of natural medicine with pharmaceuticals, the doctors said, it would have to be considered an intentional overdose.

Bea couldn't believe it was intentional. Lanie was not suicidal. She had no reason to kill herself. She was happy.

A short while later, Aunt Bea and her friend, Linda, approached Bea. "We were looking for Lanie's wallet, and we found these," Aunt Bea said. She handed her niece a bag filled with casino receipts and ATM withdrawal receipts. "We found some of them stuffed under the seat of her car," Aunt Bea added.

Bea's eyes filled with tears as the realization hit. Lanie had become so desperate that she had tried to kill herself. She had been so ashamed of what she was doing that she had told no one.

Bea walked back into her sister's room. Her heart breaking, she ran her fingers along Lanie's cheek, petting, comforting, soothing. Bea began to speak softly. "Sis, I know you're gambling again, but it's okay. There's nothing you could ever do that could make me love you less," she said. "It's going to be okay. Everything's going to be okay."

A single tear trailed down Lanie's right cheek.

Eventually, the doctors gave Lanie a shot to counteract the coma they had induced. When she opened her eyes, something wasn't right. The movement in her eyes was erratic; they were rolling from side to side. Bea could tell Lanie was no longer there, and she made the most difficult and the most humane decision she had ever made in her life.

She decided to let her beloved sister go to God.

The doctors concluded that Lanie had suffered a major brain stem stroke. Bea objected when they suggested that Lanie be placed in a nursing home, where she would live on a feeding tube for the rest of her life. Unresponsive. Trapped inside a body kept alive artificially. She knew Lanie would not want to live like that.

On June 2, 2008, while the doctors discontinued life support, Bea held her sister's hand as she took her last breath. It was a beautiful moment. Bea knew with absolute certainty that Lanie had gone to be with the Lord, and she was comforted by the fact that her sister would be happy once again. This was followed by a primal cry of pain that Bea didn't even recognize as her own voice.

A piece of her heart had shattered.

After the funeral, the determination that had always kept Bea forging ahead in life set in. Lanie had died because of a disease that people don't understand and cannot see. "Suddenly, I knew I could not be anonymous anymore," Bea said. "My whole life had been about image. No one outside of my family and those at my meetings knew I was an addict, but I learned the hard way that this disease kills people. They die in shame and silence. I knew I had to do something, but I didn't know what to do. That's when God started hitting me with two-by-fours."

The intern's words kept repeating in Bea's mind—"Did she win?" That's the first question anyone asks when they learn a person is a gambler. "They never ask, 'How much did you lose?'" Bea said. "Lanie lost everything. Lanie lost her life."

Through her own recovery, Bea had learned that her former mantra—"Dig deep. Don't quit"—was no longer appropriate. She developed a new one—"Bea still." And that's what she did for a time. She knew she had to raise awareness about this disease, but she didn't know how. Instead of rushing in full steam ahead, she slowly began to learn everything she could about gambling addiction, even as she planned a memorial to celebrate what would have been Lanie's fifty-third birthday.

"I was alone now. My parents were gone. Lanie was gone. I was grieving, and my sponsor, Jan, kept in constant touch with me," Bea said. "Lanie had always said, 'You know Mike Aikens is the love of your life.' I had always reminded her that we were both married, but as Lanie's birthday approached, I felt the need to talk to him. In thirty years, the only correspondence I had received from him was two Christmas cards and a condolence card. I looked him up and called to tell him I was coming to Pennsylvania. 'I always wanted to see the whites of your eyes once more before I die,' I said. 'I'll meet you halfway.'"

Mike no longer lived in the area, but he responded with, "I'll meet you at Negley Park."

Bea's heart skipped a beat.

She felt like she was fifteen again a few weeks later as she and Mike sat on a bench in their park listening to the Susquehanna River wind its way southward. Within five minutes, she told him about Lanie. "I sobbed," she said, "and he put his arm around me. It was so natural."

Later, they went to dinner and caught up on the past thirty years. Bea learned that Mike was divorced and that he was still the same sweet man she remembered. After dinner, they returned to their park and talked until they were interrupted by a police officer at three in the morning. "What are you two doing down there?" the officer shouted, shining his flashlight in their direction.

"We weren't doing anything, officer," Bea said, feeling like a teenager. They showed him their identification while Bea explained that they were childhood sweethearts.

The next day, she sent Mike a text and invited him to come to her Aunt Bea's house. "He adores you," Aunt Bea whispered to Bea later that day, noticing the way Mike looked at her niece. That was music to Bea's ears.

After Lanie's birthday, Bea returned to Boulder City, her heart a little lighter. Mike was strong, and she knew he would be there for her. Now, it was time to figure out what she needed to do to help others like herself and Lanie. In an effort to increase her knowledge, Bea attended a conference hosted by the National Council on Problem Gambling. When Executive Director Keith Whyte got up to speak, she paid close attention. Her plan had been to wait until she retired and then maybe join an organization. "God had other plans for me," Bea said. "Keith said that the problem with gamblers in recovery is that they are so anonymous that they are invisible. He said that most people don't know there's a problem. While he was speaking, it hit me that what we needed was a face and voice of recovery. I looked up and asked God, 'Are you talking about now?'"

The following January, Bea, who served on the board of the National Association of Women Business Owners, was driving through a rare rainstorm in Las Vegas, late for a meeting of the board. When she arrived, she noticed that something was amiss. The immediate past-president was sitting in a chair, her head in her hands, sobbing.

"She said, 'I'm a gambler, and I went through the whole treasury.' She had embezzled all of our funds," Bea explained. "That was like another of God's two-by-fours hitting me. I had never acknowledged my addiction in public. I couldn't. But in that moment, I said, 'There's no accident I'm on this board. I'm an addicted gambler in recovery. I can help.' Not one person ran from that room. The other women there were very compassionate, and I invited the past-president to a meeting. That was the beginning of the end of my business career. I knew then that God didn't want me to wait."

In Fall 2010, Bea launched Lanie's Hope. Her mantra has evolved once again from "Bea still" to "Bea the light." She is determined to bring the problem of gambling addiction from the darkness into the light.

She started with a Facebook page and then built a website, www.lanieshope. org, to raise awareness and to provide addicted gamblers with the resources they need to start a new life. Carol O'Hare, the executive director of the Nevada Council on Problem Gambling (NCPG), mentored her. Bea became a certified peer recovery coach and took any class she could find that would help her in her quest, including training on suicide prevention. She is now on the board of directors of the NCPG and serves on the National Recovery Committee and the Problem Gambling Awareness Month Committee.

"Although gambling is recognized as a mental illness by the American Psychiatric Association, insurance companies rarely cover treatment," Bea said. "My goal is to change that. And I'd like to change something else, as well. In Gamblers Anonymous, the twelve steps refer to a 'higher power of your own understanding.' I'd like to make treatment more faith-based. I love Jesus, and I want to start faith-based recovery meetings."

Today, Lanie's Hope is a nonprofit organization that provides support services for addicted gamblers and educates the community about gambling addiction. "You never, ever give money to a compulsive gambler in early recovery," Bea said, "but we do help with essentials needs, such as bus passes, food vouchers, and gas cards, so they can focus on recovery and get to work and meetings."

Bea also travels the country raising awareness through speaking engagements. "God keeps forging my path," she said. "Last year, I participated in the Suicide Prevention Coalition's Walk in Memory, Walk for Hope. At the event, they have a circle that only a family member who has lost a child, parent, or sibling to suicide can walk in. I didn't ever think I would belong in that circle. I didn't ever want to be in that circle. This year, I was the keynote speaker, and the coalition made gambling and suicide its focus. We are making progress."

In the United States, there are very few residential facilities for early recovery, but Bea wants to change that, as well. She hopes to open her own faith-based facility in the future.

Thirty-two years after they got engaged, Mike and Bea finally married in 2011. "He's a good, good man who loves the Lord," Bea says, happiness ringing in her voice. "I know in my heart Lanie sent him to me."

And through Lanie's Hope, Bea is helping addicted gamblers rebuild their lives, one person at a time.

For more information, please visit www.lanieshope.org.

BILLY RIVERS

PRISON LEADS HARDENED BIKER TO MINISTRY

"The story of grace is the Gospel of not just forgiveness, but also of redemption. God uses the weak, the ones who have failed and the ones who had run out of second chances long ago."

—Kristen McNulty, author

B illy Rivers drove his van carefully, keeping his eye on the speed limit. He did not want to attract unwanted attention. He exited Interstate110 and headed slowly toward a well-traveled dirt road near the Bridge of the Americas just across the Mexican border from Ciudad Juárez. When he reached his destination, he stopped the vehicle on the side of the road and waited while the translator he had hired jumped out.

"Be careful, man," Billy said, as he watched his cohort hurry through the brush.

Billy had been here before. Many times, in fact, but it was always the same. Adrenalin rushed through him, fueling his nervousness as he kept watch—checking his rearview mirrors and scanning the road in front of him. He knew it would take only five minutes, five minutes that were worth almost $5,000 and a quarter-ounce of eighty-two percent pure cocaine. In 1989, that was a whole lot of money for a biker, and well worth any risk.

He checked his watch, the seconds ticking by slowly as he waited. Another minute, and he would hear them coming, their movements rustling the leaves as they pushed through the brush. Billy got out of the van and walked toward the rear. He opened the doors, pushing aside two five-gallon cans of gas and several ice chests filled with soft drinks and sandwiches, so they could climb in safely.

He could hear them now, and he checked the road again before he motioned for them to hurry.

Six adults and two children.

He lined the adults along the sides of the van and directed the children to sit on the blankets he had placed by the back doors. They looked nervous, each of them, and hopeful, their dream of a new life in the United States near fulfillment.

Billy smiled reassuringly before he closed the doors.

Heaving a sigh of relief, Billy got back into the van and turned over the ignition. He made his way to Interstate 10 West without looking at a map, the familiar route ingrained in his mind. As usual, he would drive through Las Cruces, New Mexico, and then pull over in a remote area to allow his passengers to relieve themselves in the woods before driving on to Denver.

About seven miles before the Las Cruces checkpoint, Billy spotted Border Patrol and state troopers lining the side of the interstate. He knew something was very wrong when he saw men in uniforms standing outside their vehicles along the highway.

Billy began to sweat when he saw one of the men pointing in his direction.

"Oh, no," he said aloud, just before the bullets started flying, the police and federal agents aiming for his tires.

Billy slammed on the brakes, threw the van into park, and scrambled to the back to cover the children with his body.

Glass was flying.

The passengers were screaming.

The bullets kept coming.

"Get down. Get down," Billy yelled. "Cover your heads."

The barrage continued for a few seconds, but it felt like hours. When the shooting stopped, Billy had only a moment to look down before the doors of the van flew open.

The children. They weren't moving.

As he lifted his body away from them, he could see that they were dead.

He was still staring at them when he felt himself pulled roughly from the van as handcuffs were slapped around his wrists. After he was placed into a paddy wagon, Billy looked down and saw blood covering his shirt.

It was their blood.

Bile rose in his throat.

He watched in horror as their bodies were removed from the van and placed into ambulances while their parents were loaded into the paddy wagon with him. A few minutes later, the agents pulled Billy from the wagon and put him in a separate car.

He said not a word as he was driven to jail.

He couldn't.

Those kids were only ten or eleven—a boy and a girl.

Billy was hardcore, but not that hard. Tears filled his eyes as he stared numbly at the blood on his shirt.

Billy Rivers grew up in New Orleans in the 1960s in a middle-class Christian family. His father, Eddie, owned a drywall and painting business, and his mother, Nell, was a homemaker, spending much of her time cooking and cleaning and taking care of Billy and his older brother. Every evening, there was a home-cooked meal waiting when Eddie got home from work, and the family would bow their heads and thank God for their blessings before devouring seafood gumbo or fried chicken or red beans and rice.

After Nell washed the dishes, she and Eddie would sit on the couch holding hands, watching Pat Robertson or Billy Graham on a small television. Billy would sit nearby on the floor, munching on popcorn and watching with them, absorbing the values his parents were trying to instill into their children. Then the family would pray together before they went to bed.

He had a happy childhood for a while.

"At the age of twelve, I became a rebel," Billy recalls. "I started sneaking beers with my friends after school, smoking cigarettes, and smoking pot. Growing up on the streets of New Orleans wasn't easy, and I got into a lot of fights."

Nell and Eddie worried that Billy was going down a bad road, but in the sixties, all parents had that fear. American teenagers were evolving from sweet, innocent children into young people their parents did not understand. Many parents like Billy's helplessly watched the traditional values they had instilled into their children being replaced with rebellion, disrespect, uninhibited behavior. Rock idols, like Jimi Hendrix and Janis Joplin, were changing the culture. Sex, drugs, and rock and roll were much more appealing to youngsters than Billy Graham and Pat Robertson, and much more influential.

When he was thirteen, Billy watched an acquaintance stick a needle in his arm and shoot heroin into his veins. He observed with interest the smile that accompanied that first rush, and when the drug was offered to him, he did not hesitate. "I was just taken away," he recalled. "I had never experienced anything that made me feel that good. There was such excitement in doing it."

Blissfully unaware of the danger, a few days later, Billy shot up cocaine.

"That was the end of Billy," he said. "I was off and running."

On the days Billy wanted to feel mellow, he ran heroin. When he wanted his world to be bright lights and glamour, he ran coke. "Cocaine was the ultimate high for me, and it was my preference," he said. "But heroin was more plentiful back then. Heroin grabbed ahold of me and didn't let go."

By the time he was fourteen, Billy had developed a $300-per-week habit. His parents had worked hard, saved their money, and invested $24,000 to buy their home. As a young teenager, Billy spent that amount of money on dope in a year.

"My parents knew what I was doing, and it broke their hearts," Billy said, "but I was too far gone to care. I didn't care about much except getting high and feeling good."

Three days before he turned sixteen, Billy married his pregnant girlfriend, Judy, and soon became a father. His parents helped him buy a mobile home, and he moved to Pearl River, Louisiana, a rural area about forty-five miles north of New Orleans. Even the responsibility of being a father to his beautiful daughter, Alicia, didn't stop Billy from using the drugs that by now were as necessary to his well-being as breathing. The marriage lasted six and a half years before his drug use caused his divorce.

After a brief relationship with another woman, Billy learned he would become a father again. He did not meet his second child, Sh'Dawn, until she was two years old, and he did not see her again until she was fifteen.

A few years later, Billy met his second wife, Linda, and moved with her to Reno, Nevada, to take a job in construction. It was there that Billy became involved in a motorcycle gang in California. "It started at a racetrack," Billy explained. "I had a Harley, and I was winning a lot of races. A lot of gang members hung out at the track, and we became friends. I had no hesitation whatsoever when I was invited to join."

Through the gang, Billy experienced a brotherhood he had not known before. Theirs was a close-knit family where everyone took care of everyone else, with a bit of violence and a lot of drugs and illegal activity thrown into the mix. Billy became a one-percenter—the one percent of gang members who have total dedication to the lifestyle, tagged by gang members and law enforcement as outlaws, and he wore his patch and colors proudly. That lifestyle came with a hefty price tag, though.

Linda left him, taking their baby son, Dalton, with her. "I've only seen my son three times, and he's twenty-two now," Billy said. "He was raised with total hate in his heart for me because of my lifestyle. I made bad decisions back then, and they were costly ones. Now I can only pray that he will forgive me."

Billy's role in the gang was to smuggle illegal aliens out of Mexico into the United States. He had made numerous trips over the years, transporting eight illegals each time, before that fateful day in 1989 when the FBI, ATF, New Mexico State Police, and Border Patrol, mistakenly believing he was transporting drugs and guns, began shooting at his tires.

"They had no idea that the club was transporting illegals," Billy explained.

Initially, Billy was charged with two counts of second-degree murder and a variety of RICO (Racketeer Influenced and Corrupt Organizations Act) charges. The federal prosecutor in the case, incensed by the death of the children, avowed that he would not sleep until Billy Rivers did one hundred sixty-five years in prison. One year later, Billy stood before a judge to learn his fate.

"I was waiting to be sentenced to one hundred sixty-five years," Billy remembers. "Instead, the judge said, 'The charges of murder are dismissed. You did not take the lives of those children.'"

Billy was shocked. He felt responsible. Their lifeless bodies lying beneath his, their blood on his shirt, haunted him.

The RICO charges were also dismissed. Ultimately, Billy pled guilty to bringing illegal aliens into the country and was sentenced to a mandatory eight years in federal prison.

Billy entered prison with his gang attitude still firmly in place, ready to fight at the drop of a hat as he had always done, but before long, he found himself in the role of protecting the younger men who weren't as tough. "There's a lot that goes on in prison," he said. "Everyone wants what you have—socks, snacks, whatever. I would put the younger guys' stuff in my locker and tell the older guys, 'I'll kill you while you sleep if you try to take their stuff.'"

The older guys believed him. Billy had a reputation, and they didn't mess with him.

In prison, the biker, who had spent so much time living outside of the law, began to think about changing his life. Three times each week, prisoners could exit their cells and attend church services. At first, Billy wasn't interested, but he did notice that the Christian prisoners always came back happier. Moments of happiness are fleeting in a six-by-eight cell, and he began thinking about his mother and father, who had gained such peace and happiness from their evening rituals and prayers.

"I started remembering that my parents had never lied to me, not once, so why would they lie about Jesus?" Billy said. "Sometimes the preacher in prison would come talk to me. I told him, 'If I can't see Jesus or feel Him or touch Him, I'm not gonna believe in Him.' The preacher said, 'I'm not going to give up on you.' That impressed me. I started attending services, partly as a way of getting out of my cell three times each week and partly because of that preacher."

Billy served his sentence in federal prison for the most part uneventfully, although he spent a lot of time thinking about his childhood and the choices he had made that had brought him to this point. After his release, he was sent to Gulfport, Mississippi, to serve three more years for skipping bail on a prior burglary arrest.

It was in Gulfport that everything changed for Billy. One day, the Christian Motorcyclists Association (CMA) and Bill Glass Ministries hosted a Weekend of Champions at the prison. The members of motorcycle ministry were allowed to ride their bikes into the prison to display them for the inmates. Three hundred inmates were invited to participate. Billy was excited when he learned that he would be included in this unusual event.

"I remember standing there, watching, as Don Johnson from Cullman, Alabama, pulled in and cut his bike off," Billy said. "He looked at me. He was staring. An inmate said, 'That guy is staring at you.' I've got a convict mentality, so I walked across the yard toward him, and I said, 'Mister, I don't appreciate you staring at me.' Don looked at me harder and said, 'Jesus Christ spoke to my heart about you and not the other two hundred ninety-nine people in this yard, and I'd appreciate it if you would be quiet and listen to what I have to tell you.' That was a Saturday morning. Don spent the rest of the day with me. He came back Sunday morning and talked with me some more. That day, I accepted Jesus Christ into my life. God used a motorcycle and a bunch of bikers to touch my heart. In His wisdom, He knew that was the only thing that would work."

Soon after, Billy received a letter from a man named John Capitano, who was the president of the New Orleans chapter of the CMA at the time. Don had told John about the biker he had met in prison.

"Johnny started writing me letters," Billy recalled. "In them, he stated that he didn't know me, but he loved me. I was thinking, 'How can he love me?' I thought it was crazy, but when I got released, I arranged to meet Johnny and his wife, Callie, at a restaurant in Picayune, Mississippi. Johnny opened his wallet and handed me sixty dollars. He told me to buy some new clothes. I hesitated, then asked him what he wanted in return. 'For you to understand the love of Jesus Christ,' was all he said. From then on, every time I put on the clothes I bought with Johnny's money, I could hear his voice. That made such an impression on me."

With nowhere left to go, Billy moved in with his parents in Gulfport to start his new life. One afternoon, he borrowed his mother's car and went to a CMA meeting. "A CMA member walked up to me. I informed him that I had just been released from prison. 'I'm an ex-heroin user. I heard y'all like people like me,' I said. He said, 'Yes, we do.'"

Billy joined the association, finding acceptance and love for the right reasons this time, and moved back to New Orleans. Men like Kerry Gibson and John Ogdon Jr. helped guide his path back to righteousness. One year later, James and Rita Johnston, pastors who worked in a prison outreach ministry in Tulsa, Oklahoma, ordained and licensed Billy in the Glory Refuge Church. The biker had never been happier. Whereas once his mission had been to serve himself and the gang in which he had found a home, now he focused on serving God and his fellow man.

Billy served as chaplain of the New Orleans chapter of the CMA for the next two years. He was voted president of the association the following year. It wasn't long before his story began getting attention. It was a tale worthy of none other than Pat Robertson, the minister who had spent so many hours talking to his family through a television when Billy was a child. Pat decided to make a film of Billy's story for the 700 Club titled, *A Hardened Biker Switches Gears* (available on YouTube).

"After Pat called, I'm sitting here thinking I had nothing to offer but being a gang member, a thief, a liar, a drug addict. I had nothing to offer but trash. But then it was like the Lord said, 'Billy, I can take dirt from the ground and make whatever I want out of it.' I realized I needed to make the film."

During the airing of the film, five hundred seventy-four people called the show and gave their life to Christ. For the first time in his life, Billy realized he had a purpose, that perhaps everything in his life had happened so that God could use him to touch others, to bring them from the darkness into the light.

Today, Billy is a painting contractor in New Orleans like his father once was, "and a Christian like my dad," he's quick to add. He married the love of his life, Donna, seven years ago. "My wife is a strong part of my ministry," he says. "She's a great prayer warrior. God knew I would need a strong woman, and I am so grateful He sent Donna to me."

Billy spends his weekdays working to provide for his family and his weekends sharing his story of hope to people across the world. The bearded, gray-haired biker with a thin build and fifty-three tattoos is not the stereotypical minister, but the life he has lived, the experiences that turned him into such a devoted follower of Christ, have helped him reach people who may not otherwise listen to a traditional minister.

Those people include the homeless who live underneath Interstate 10 in New Orleans, hopeless people mostly ignored by the thousands of residents who drive the side streets that run parallel to the interstate. The men and women sit on the ground, knapsacks or garbage bags that house all of their belongings by their sides, each with his or her own story of desperation. While most people just turn their heads and look away, Billy and Donna can't do that.

Together, they serve the homeless as often as they can, along with other ministries and individuals who share the same passion. They set up tables under the interstate close to the New Orleans Mission, tables filled with pans of steaming jambalaya and sandwiches, made by men and women who donate their hearts, time, and energy for this cause. They feed the homeless and pray with them, while they distribute toothbrushes, toothpaste, clothes, blankets, soap, and Bibles. "It's incredible," Billy said. "We get so many donations from schools and churches that sometimes my garage is so full, I can't get my motorcycle out."

Billy now lives a life he would have never envisioned for himself, a life filled with love, laughter, and the knowledge that miracles can happen to anyone. He knows this because he received his own personal miracle—redemption—and with it a new life.

"When I tell people who I was and who I am now, it gives them hope. Many people think they have done such bad things that God will never forgive them. I tell them not to believe that lie. If God can forgive me for the things I've done, for those children in that van, he can forgive anyone. When I see people give their lives to God, I get such a feeling of thankfulness. It's the greatest feeling I could ever imagine."

While Billy was serving his time in federal prison, it was his job to collect the dirty clothes from the prisoners on death row and to bring them food. His cell was located two steel doors away from death row.

"I was on death row every day," Billy said. "Now I talk to audiences of up to four thousand people about love and hope and salvation. I can't believe this is my life now. The Lord truly works in mysterious ways. I am a blessed man."

For more information, please e-mail Billy at billyrivers794@gmail.com or visit his website at www.ahardenedbikerswitchesgears.com.

GEORGE MILLS

"It's funny, because we all read history and we think, 'Oh, I would have risen up, I would have fought, I would have been an abolitionist,' And I tell them, 'No, you wouldn't have. If you would have, you'd be doing that right now. You know trafficking exists, you've heard of it, but you don't want to look."

—Tim Ballard, founder of Operation Underground Railroad

George Mills placed the heroin onto the spoon, careful not to drop any. He looked around for a syringe, then poured some peroxide over the needle, hoping that would do the trick. He didn't want to deal with another infection. He drew water into the syringe and then released a small amount onto the heroin. Satisfied he had enough, he pushed the plunger down to remove the excess water. He reached for his lighter and picked up the spoon, years of practice preventing him from spilling a drop. At twenty years old, he had mastered this art.

After heating the mixture, George set the spoon down to give his dope a minute to cool. He looked at his arms and hands, searching for a good vein. There were none, only scar tissue that had grown over his usual spots of injection. He searched his legs, same problem. His veins were blown. Desperate now, he leaned down to check his feet. He was in luck.

Smiling, George dabbed a small piece of cotton on the spoon to soak up the liquid. He stuck the needle about halfway into the cotton and slowly drew back on the plunger. When he had enough, he placed the cotton ball on the table. It would be good for another hit or two later. He held the syringe up to the light, pushing on the plunger until the powdery mixture was close enough to the tip of the needle, then rubbed his foot for a moment to increase circulation. Holding the syringe at a forty-five degree angle, George guided the needle into his vein, emptying the syringe and then pulling the plunger back up. There was blood. Good. He hadn't missed the vein.

Leaning back on the couch, George waited.

And then it came.

He looked at the girl beside him. She smiled, her eyes bleary, her arms as marked as his.

She had brought him the heroin. He wondered what she had done to get it, but then the thought was gone.

Back then he didn't care.

Growing up in the sixties in Dearborn, Michigan, a suburb of Detroit, George Mills was like many other teenagers who grew up in that era—rebellious. His father, George Sr., earned a respectable living for the family as a pediatrician. His mother, Gail, a homemaker, enjoyed taking care of her family. They lived in Dearborn Country Club Estates, and most of their neighbors were doctors or Ford Motor Company executives. George had three brothers—Steve, Scott, and Jeff—and he was the oldest, the leader of the pack.

"My mom lived in a house with five males," George said. "And we were alpha males. Even our pets were males."

Although he played sports like his brothers did, George was more into music. In the late sixties, music was evolving swiftly, from the crooners who had wooed the previous generation into more drug-influenced, guitar-driven rock that spoke to teenagers like music had never done before. George wanted to be a part of that.

He began playing the trumpet but later switched to electric bass. He loved being around musicians and played in local bands, rock and roll mostly, but as he got older, his taste evolved to progressive rock and jazz. George embraced sex, drugs, and rock and roll from a very early age, much to the dismay of his parents, who had no idea what to do with him.

"I was thirteen years old the first time I injected Seconal," he said. "Before long, I was doing all the reds, yellows, and Quaaludes I could get my hands on. A lot of our parents were doctors, so it was easy. Then it was coke and heroin. Even early on, I always preferred injectable drugs."

George was sixteen the first time he was arrested. George Sr. had a property on Hilton Head Island, and George, without permission, decided to go stay there for a while. After breaking into a few drug stores and doctors' offices to steal barbiturates and whatever other drugs he could find to feed his growing habit, he got caught.

"I was sent to the Juvenile Evaluation Center in Greenville, South Carolina, for a pre-sentencing evaluation. I thought it was an interesting facility. If we got into a fight, they let us put on boxing gloves and go at it after dinner. I won more than I lost," George recalled.

George was soon sent back to Michigan and ordered to see a psychiatrist. He was also enrolled in an alternative high school that allowed students to smoke, which George liked, and he eventually graduated.

"I partied my way through that school," he said. "Detroit was only fifteen miles away, and you could get good quality heroin there. Cocaine was also coming down in price at that time, so freebasing became another good way for me to get high. I liked coke."

George enrolled in community college soon after graduation, but his drug use was getting out of control. "By the time I was twenty-one, I was really strung out," he explained. "I owed money to people, I had infections in my arms. It got bad."

Realizing he needed help, George called his father. Praying that his son had finally hit rock bottom and would embrace recovery, George Sr. sent him to a drug treatment facility, located in Deer Park, Texas. "I remember it was a hundred degrees," George said. "I was carrying my bass and a suitcase, and then I was wearing a blue gown. I met Carrie Hamilton, Carol Burnett's daughter, at that facility, and we went through treatment together."

After completing the program, George, clean for the first time in years, got a job in Houston. He was arrested soon after for possession of cocaine and sentenced to ten years of probation.

In Texas, George met Cindy Armstrong at a dance studio he managed, and they fell in love. After a brief courtship, the couple married. Cindy's father owned a restaurant in Alvin, and he asked George to come to work for him. "After a few years, he offered to let me buy half the restaurant because he wanted to expand," George said. "We opened a cafeteria near the NASA area, but then the space shuttle Challenger exploded, and business went downhill. We had to close it."

George soon decided to try his hand at real estate and did very well for a while. He and Cindy had two children, Shayla and Taryn. Cindy did not like the fact that George still injected drugs, but she dealt with it as best she could. During those years, George was arrested several more times but always managed to avoid prison. Then in 1989, he was arrested on three felony counts and remanded to the Texas Department of Corrections.

"They gave me the option to go to Cenikor or go to prison. I chose prison," George said. Cenikor, a long-term residential drug rehabilitation program, which was located in Texas, had a reputation for being tough. George was simply not interested and was sent instead to the L.V. Hightower Unit in Dayton, Texas. He was sentenced to five years on each count to run concurrently.

"I always got religion in prison," George said. "I was saved one minute and backsliding the next. It was more like, 'God, help me out of this,' with no attempt on my part to actually live like a Christian."

George served six months and six days and was released. He tried to live a good life, and it worked for a while, but then he returned to his old habits. He and Cindy soon divorced. Two years later, he was arrested again and sent to the Texas State Penitentiary at Huntsville to serve a nine-year sentence.

"I was a trustee there and worked in night administration and then the motor pool, washing and fueling vehicles and even driving them outside of the prison," George said.

Five days after his release in May 1994, George was arrested for unauthorized use of a vehicle, but this time, he had earned habitual offender status. He was facing fifty-five years, basically the rest of his life, in prison.

"I realized while we were trying to negotiate a plea bargain that the results in my life would always be the same unless I changed," he said. "I got very lucky. In the middle of the trial, they changed judges. The new judge offered me the opportunity to go to Cenikor. I jumped on it. He warned me that if I didn't complete the program, I would spend fifty-five years in prison."

On August 4, 1994, George was released. Two men in a van picked him up and drove him to the same facility in Deer Park where he had spent time years before. It had become a Cenikor facility. "It was a two-and-a-half- to three-year program and very tough," George said. "At first, I didn't think I would make it."

As part of the program, residents must get a job, so George went to work at Screen Images in Houston. It was located in an area of the city that George knew very well. He had a lot of old friends there.

"After a few months at Cenikor, something strange happened. I was at work one day, and I looked out the window. My vision had changed. All of those people on those streets looked dead to me, dirty, like a herd of cattle crowding around the dope man. That was the moment I really began to put effort into changing," George said.

Started in 1967 by a group of inmates at the Colorado State Penitentiary,

Cenikor was founded on the principle that former addicts could better identify with and help other addicts than those unfamiliar with substance abuse. They developed a program that has proved to be one of the most successful substance abuse programs ever designed. "It's tough," George said. "You don't get babied, but you learn to take responsibility for your actions, for your life. And most importantly, you are given the tools to eradicate your addiction."

George's attitude and behavior changed so radically over the next eighteen months that Cenikor offered him the position of resident-in-training. By the start of 1996, George was a changed man, a man who loved the Lord. Cenikor asked him to move to Baton Rouge to help run an outreach office they had opened there the year before—the Leo Butler Community Center.

"I really thought I could do this, but back then I was somewhat egotistical," George said. "A month after I was there, we got our first $100 donation. It was tough going for a while. In the beginning, we provided outreach services that made long-term residential treatment in Texas available to the residents of Louisiana."

George had a knack for business, though, and before long the donations began coming in from community organizations—the Irene W. and C.B. Pennington Foundation, Latter & Blum, and Baton Rouge Area Foundation.

"Mike Barnett, a colonel with the East Baton Rouge Parish Sheriff's Office, called me one day and said, 'George, I've got good news and bad news. The Penningtons aren't giving you $50,000. They're giving you $100,000.' I couldn't believe it. I knew how many lives could be saved with that money," George said.

In 1998, George, who had regularly attended church since his recovery, met Shira, and he soon fell in love. "She is sometimes shocked by my past, but she is more concerned about my present and my future," George said. "Fortunately for me, she loved who I was. She didn't focus on what I was."

Two years later, the couple married. Shira had three children from a previous marriage, and George, who had not seen his own children in many years, embraced the role of fatherhood for the first time. "I tried to find my kids, but Cindy had moved with them to California after our divorce, and I had no clue where to look," he explained.

In 1999, the Irene W. and C.B. Pennington Foundation donated $1 million, and then Charlie Lamar, founder of the Charles Lamar Family Foundation, donated $275,000 toward the building of a large facility that could better serve people from all over Louisiana. George, now regional vice president, oversaw the purchase, financing, design, renovation, licensing, and fundraising of the project.

"It took eighteen months to renovate," George said. "In 2001, we licensed the first beds, and we've grown to two hundred thirty beds. It's now the largest Cenikor facility, and here, we've helped thousands of addicts recover and return to society as productive citizens."

By 2004, George was finally released from probation and parole. For the first time in many years, the weight of his former life was lifted. "I'm sorry my dad didn't live to see this," he said. "He passed away six months before I was released from prison. I think he would have finally had a chance to be proud of me. My mom certainly is, but it took her a while. I remember the first time I went to visit her she didn't realize how much I had changed. Before we went to sleep, she grabbed her purse and her keys and hid them. I had to smile. I knew then that it would take a lot of work to earn back her trust, but eventually I did."

Through hard work and dedication, George had earned the trust of many— his family, Cenikor, the Baton Rouge community, and the substance abusers who counted on him to show them the way to a better life. For the next six years, he was happy, happier than he had ever been, but something was still missing—his children. He wanted to meet them again, to tell them that he loved them and that he was sorry for his life choices that had robbed them of a good father.

In 2010, he found Shayla and Taryn on Myspace. "I sent Shayla a message that said, 'If your mother's first name is Cindy, I am probably your father. I would like to meet you.' Initially I spoke with Shayla and then Taryn. It was uncomfortable at first because Shayla barely remembered me, and Taryn didn't even know I was her father," George said. "It's great now, though. I have two grandchildren and one more on the way."

That same year, George won the John W. Barton Sr. Excellence in Nonprofit Management Award from the Baton Rouge Area Foundation for the work he had done through Cenikor. In 2011, he was promoted to vice president of Business Development for the Cenikor Foundation.

George continued in that position for several years, happy with the progress he had made in his life. Then in 2014, George began having difficulty walking because of a problem with his left foot. One evening, a friend suggested he visit a prayer room to pray with others for healing. George thought that was a good idea, and when he arrived, he told the receptionist why he needed prayer. He went into a room where three people were waiting to pray with him. While they were praying, one of the men looked at George and said, "God is going to move you in a different direction. You need to embrace that."

Three months later, at a prayer meeting at Healing Place Church, another woman told him the same thing. George realized this was not a coincidence. The Lord was preparing him for something.

Not long after, George received a call from the office of the founder of Trafficking Hope and Hope House. "Lee Dominique asked me if I would become president of Hope House. I prayed about it and realized this must be what God was nudging me toward," George said. He made his decision and resigned from Cenikor, giving up his hope of eventual retirement in the process.

Hope House is a not-for-profit organization, cofounded by Lee and his wife, Laura, dedicated to providing services for rescued victims of sexual slavery and human traffickers. "Human trafficking is a $150.2 billion industry worldwide," George said. "It includes everything from prostitution, escort services, and pornography to strip clubs, massage parlors, cam rooms, and chat rooms. In Louisiana, we have Interstate 20 to the north and Interstates 10 and 12 to the south. These are major corridors for human traffickers."

Through the use of force, fraud, and coercion, human traffickers lure victims into the sex trade—the more victims they have, the more money they make. In today's technologically advanced world, the trafficking of young women and men has become much easier. For example, a plethora of webpages exists throughout the Internet where young ladies and men can advertise their services—everything from name, age, and weight to what sexual acts they will perform, their experience level, and the cost. Unbelievably, some pages even allow customer ratings to be posted—disgusting comments designed to further humiliate and denigrate these young people.

George says that luring young girls, many of them teenagers, into the sex trade is as easy as friending them on Facebook or meeting on a dating website. "Recruiters solicit with promises of money or drugs. They sometimes coerce their victims by threatening to send naked photos of them out over the Internet. They can spot vulnerabilities and use them to their advantage. It's a scary world out there for young women. I know. I experienced it back when I was an addict. It was nothing for a girl to trade sex to feed her addiction. The same thing goes on in the porn industry. So many people watch porn, and they have no idea what's going on behind the scenes when the cameras aren't rolling. Many of these girls are forced to be there through one means or another."

Traffickers seem harmless at first. A simple date with a recruiter can result in a forced sexual act. Fear is a huge component of the trafficker's success. Moving victims around from city to city also works in favor of the trafficker. It becomes harder for victims to run away.

"I've dealt with victims first trafficked as young as eight years old. People need to be aware of this," George said. "We live in the United States of America, and in this country, the slave trade is bigger than ever. Parents need to monitor their children's use of social media because predators are out there twenty-four hours each day searching for their next victim. Through our visual no-holds-barred media, we are sending the wrong messages to our young people. The filters have moved in our society, and so many young people are paying dearly for that."

Teenagers are the biggest target. One of the largest porn sites on the Web recently reported that the most frequently searched word on its site was "teen."

Through fear, false promises, and low self-esteem, many victims become brainwashed into feeling affection for their trafficker. One victim shared with George, "All my life I've been called 'fat.' Now men pay for me."

Hope House, located in a rural wooded area of Louisiana, provides residential services and healing to trafficking victims. Victims are not only offered housing, but they are also provided educational opportunities, counseling services, and holistic services in an effort to heal their bodies, hearts, and minds.

"There are six pillars of transformation—faith, physical health, behavioral health, life skills, education, and workforce—but faith is the foundation of the program." George said. "Many of the girls who come to us don't know how to obtain a driver's license or open a checking account or even shop for groceries. We teach them about nutrition and hygiene, how to dress and act appropriately—all the things their traffickers robbed from them."

Victims come from all walks of life. One young woman at Hope House was a college student when she was recruited. Another had spent time in twenty-three foster homes by the time she was eighteen. One young woman stated that she had never had a job that was not on her back.

"It's hard to change their perception of life," George said. "It takes time, and that's why this program is a mandatory nine to eighteen months. We have to teach them that value is not an hourly rate. It's hard to convince them that making ten- to-twelve dollars per hour is a good thing when they've been making $300 per hour. Even though they receive only a small percentage of that money, they still value themselves at $300 per hour. Our job is to make each girl feel valuable as one of God's children."

In September 2015, Hope House merged with Trafficking Hope Louisiana, an anti-sex trafficking organization that raises awareness and educates the public about this insidious problem. George serves as president of the combined organization.

"Like so many of the people I try to help, it all started out as fun for me. I identify with rebellion. I had self-esteem issues. I started out getting high now and then. It turned real ugly before I knew it. That's the way it is for many trafficking victims," George said.

Today, George sits behind the desk in his office a transformed man, his face unusually smooth and unmarked for an ex-drug addict. His eyes are kind, gentle. His long sleeves cover the scars that still run up his arms. Those scars serve as a reminder of where he's been and keep him motivated to help others escape the life that he understands all too well. His heart is filled with gratitude each time another young woman regains her strength and self-esteem and graduates from Hope House, ready to face the world, armed with the tools she needs to live her life with dignity.

And each time, George bows his head and thanks the Lord.

For more information, please visit www.traffickinghopela.org.

MORE ROCK BOTTOM AND BACK HEROES

DANNY TREJO

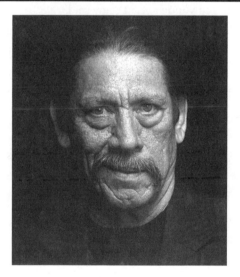

D anny Trejo's life is mirrored in his face. Pockmarks, crags, and weathered skin depict the scars he earned at an early age on the streets of Los Angeles, and then later in prison. He looks tough, for sure; he has banked on that for decades. But despite that toughness, humor dances in his dark brown eyes, and his smile radiates warmth and kindness. His is an interesting face, a face full of character that earned him a place in movie history.

The son of Alice and Dan Trejo, Danny could have led a normal life. His mom, a homemaker, dedicated herself to her family. His father, a construction worker, was a disciplinarian, but that wasn't so bad. Danny needed a firm hand. It was his Uncle Gilbert who led him astray.

Gilbert was flashy and fun. He was also a professional thief, who enjoyed showing his nephew the wads of cash he stole from the local liquor store. Dan tried to keep control of his son, but Gilbert was the one who had Danny's full attention.

"Growing up, I started using drugs at a young age," Danny said.

When he was eight, Gilbert introduced him to marijuana. The young boy wanted to be cool like his uncle, and he quickly mastered the art of getting high. Gilbert also introduced Danny to boxing. He stressed the importance of being able to fight. Gilbert knew that Danny would need to be able to defend himself if he was going to hang around with him. Danny proved early on that he had a strong jaw, that he could take the punches Gilbert threw with lightning speed.

Gilbert gave Danny his first fix at the age of thirteen, and the teenager soon became addicted to heroin. His uncle had progressed from robbing liquor stores to robbing banks, from using his fists to brandishing a weapon, and sometimes he took Danny along for the ride. Most of the time, Danny didn't know what was happening. Gilbert would tell him to wait in the car they had stolen, and then he'd come running out of his target du jour with another stack of bills. The money was great, but the rush of committing the crime and getting away with it was even better.

When he was fifteen, Danny was arrested for the first time, and he was sent to juvenile hall on drug-related charges. When he got out, Gilbert was waiting, and they picked up where they had left off.

For the next eleven years, prison became a revolving door, as Danny graduated from the California Youth Authority to hardcore facilities—Folsom State Prison, San Quentin, and Salinas Valley State Prison in Soledad. Gilbert's training and Danny's muscular physique served him well. Even hardened criminals knew that Danny Trejo had fists that could make you wish you had stayed in your cell that day. At only five feet six inches tall, Danny boxed his way to respect, eventually winning the boxing championship in the lightweight and welterweight divisions at San Quentin.

Although Danny had learned the control necessary to box in a ring, his fights within the prison walls often spiraled out of control. In May 1968, while he was serving his time in Soledad, a riot broke out. Danny threw a rock at a group of inmates—a rock that hit a guard in the head. Danny was sent to solitary confinement. As he entered the hole, Danny became afraid for the first time in his life. He knew there was a possibility he could go to the gas chamber if he were found guilty of assaulting the guard.

Over the next few months, the darkness, the solitude, the fear, started eating away at the tough exterior he had so carefully cultivated. "I made a deal with God in solitary," he said. "I told Him, 'If You let me die with dignity, I'll say Your name every day, and I'll do everything I can to help my fellow man.'"

God heard his prayer. After spending five months in the hole, the charges against Danny were dropped. Thousands of people resided at the prison, but not one said they saw Danny throw that rock. There were simply no witnesses to the assault.

When Danny was released, Gilbert was waiting at the gate, but Danny refused to take the ride this time.

He also honored his deal with God. Danny soon began to volunteer as a court liaison for young men who had been arrested on drug and alcohol charges. Through the Narcotics Prevention Program, he counseled boys in juvenile halls who were traveling the same road he had once traveled. He warned them about what could happen. They believed him. He personified an ex-convict.

"When I got out of prison, I dedicated my life to helping other people," he said. "Anything good that has happened to me is a result of me helping someone else."

His film career is a fine example of that. In 1985, while helping a young man who was struggling with his recovery, Danny wound up on a movie set. A screenwriter on the set had once spent time in San Quentin, and he remembered that Danny was a great boxer. He asked Danny to train some of the actors on the set. After Director Andrei Konchalovsky watched Danny train Eric Roberts, the star of *Runaway Train*, the director pitted Danny against Roberts in the movie.

Danny quickly became the go-to villain in Hollywood. The man who had once slept on a cold floor in a dark hole, fearing death as punishment for his crimes, soon had a career as an outlaw, complete with a paycheck and fans. Throughout his career, Danny acted in almost two hundred movies, most notably *Desperado*, *Con Air*, *Heat*, *Once Upon a Time in Mexico*, *Spy Kids*, and *Machete*, which cemented his fame.

Even those who don't know his name know the distinctive face that could inspire fear in the movie industry's most vicious killers.

Danny has now spent more than four decades sober. The physical scars from the life he once led are still visible. The emotional scars are there, as well, simmering just below the surface. "We have two ways to learn in life," he said. "We can get burned and share our own scars, or we can look at someone else's scars and learn from their story." Danny's story has helped hundreds of young men avoid a life behind bars.

Always willing to contribute his name to a worthy cause, Danny recently narrated a DVD companion to *Rock Bottom and Back*. "After a life of drugs, alcohol, and crime, I hit rock bottom in Soledad Prison, a place I thought I would never leave," he said. "Instead, it was where I began to rebuild and come back."

And whenever the opportunity arises, Danny still extends a helping hand to those in need of direction. "Restoring classic cars, it's a passion of mine," he said. "I enjoy getting hold of a used, abused, or broken-down junker and then cleaning it up inside and out, bringing it back to its original condition or better. I also have a passion for restoring broken lives back to their original condition. I can tell you from personal experience that restoration of the mind, body, and soul is possible. Miracles do happen."

Danny is living proof of that.

For more information, please visit www.dannytrejo.net.

HENRY TOBIAS

Finding shelter from the storm

The French Quarter in New Orleans, famous for its unique cuisine and infamous for its bawdy nightlife, was the catalyst for young Henry Tobias to become immersed in a world filled with alcohol, drugs, and strippers. Even though the Quarter was not far from where he grew up, no one who knew the young man would have ever thought that he would have chosen that path. He had been a good student, an athlete, a leader.

When Henry was three years old, his mother shot and killed his father. Henry recalls little about his parents other than what he has been told. His father, a truck driver, was a humble man with a loving heart. His mother, a social worker, was less affectionate with Henry and his sisters. She helped provide for the family and took care of the necessities, but she was not a nurturer. Then they were gone—his father killed, his mother sent to prison.

Henry's godparents, Noble Johnson and Frances Pruitt, adopted him and gave the young boy a good life. Henry attended Catholic school, played in the school band, and ran track. After he graduated from high school, he enrolled in college to learn hotel and restaurant management. He began working as a back waiter at Mr. B's Bistro, a five-star restaurant located on Royal Street.

"In the French Quarter, I lost all sense of right and wrong," Henry said. "I could have never imagined such a lifestyle—beautiful women everywhere, free-flowing alcohol, and drugs, of course. It didn't take long for cocaine to become my drug of choice. The French Quarter is the devil's playhouse."

Every evening after work, Henry would meet other waiters, bartenders, and chefs for drinks at strip clubs, and he would end up partying the rest of the night. All of his dreams and goals disappeared in his drug-enhanced euphoria. He thought he was having the time of his life.

When Hurricane Katrina struck, Henry's world was turned upside down. His sister Daisy Williams passed away in the Superdome, which had been designated by then-Mayor Ray Nagin as a shelter of last resort. His sister Annette Tobias died at the New Orleans Convention Center, where thousands of people sheltered after the city filled with water. Henry's home flooded, and within a week of the storm, Henry, like so many others, found himself on a bus headed for a new life.

"It was numbing for me. I lost my sisters. I lost my home. I can't even describe what it was like," he said.

For the next few years, Henry moved a lot—Mississippi, Georgia, California—never settling in one place for very long. He continued partying, using drugs and alcohol to quash his pain. After moving to New York, he enrolled in culinary school and eventually earned his degree. By the time he graduated, he had been running from his past for ten years.

In 2014, Henry returned to his hometown.

"When I got back to New Orleans, I realized that it was time to get off my high horse, so to speak," he said. "I had accomplished a lot in New York, but I knew I needed to commit myself to the Lord. I needed to change."

Henry did just that. He stopped doing all of the things that had consumed his life before. He joined Marine & Mt. Moriah Ministries, a two hundred-year-old ministry rooted in service to the Greater New Orleans area. He began to serve God and his fellow man.

Henry now teaches Sunday school and Bible study classes while studying to be ordained as a deacon. He works at the New Orleans Mission, helping to raise money for the homeless of New Orleans. He knows better than most how important home is, and he now dedicates his life to helping others find their way to a home of their own.

For more information, please visit www.neworleansmission.org.

KRISTEN MADDOX

LIFE AFTER DEATH—THE WILL TO GIVE AGAIN

Kristen Maddox's life was surrounded with drugs from as far back as she can remember. Her mother and stepfather were addicts, and their home resembled a pharmacy, with people coming and going at all hours of the day and night. When she was fourteen, Kristen started experimenting with drugs and began having a sexual relationship with her boyfriend. Before long, she discovered she was pregnant. Her mother discussed Kristen's options with her—adoption, abortion, or becoming a mother. Kristen decided to keep her baby. She married his father, and at the age of fifteen, she gave birth to a beautiful baby boy. She named him Ricky.

The next year, Kristen discovered she was pregnant again. She had graduated from high school early and had enrolled in college. Between her newborn son, her husband, and school, she was simply overwhelmed. "This time, I decided to have an abortion," she said. "It seemed so simple, like a good solution, but it changed me as a person."

Kristen was not prepared for the sadness and the guilt she experienced after the abortion, so she turned to drugs to soothe the pain. At eighteen, she went to jail for the first time. When she was released from prison, she became pregnant, and nine months later she gave birth to a baby girl she named Krisie.

Kristen loved being a mother to her children, but she couldn't stop living the lifestyle that now consumed her. The next eight years became a vicious cycle—addiction, abortion, incarceration.

Then she discovered she was pregnant again. When she went to get an abortion, she accidentally walked through the wrong door and found herself in a pregnancy crisis center. "It was divine intervention," she said. "I learned that I was not ridding myself of an undeveloped mass of tissue. This was a real baby."

Kristen did not terminate the pregnancy.

Two months later, she was raped. "While it was happening, I could feel his arm pressing against my stomach, and I was so afraid that something would happen to my baby," she said. "I knew then that I had to get out of this life I was living."

Kristen called her probation officer and asked him to arrest her. She knew that she could leave a rehabilitation facility if she wanted to, but she would not be able to escape a cell. Her probation officer brought her back to jail when she was four months pregnant.

"I cried out to God while I was in jail," she said. "I knew how I badly needed help."

God answered her prayer, and Kristen was freed from the bondage of drugs that had been worse than the reality of any jail in which she had ever been incarcerated. Two months before her daughter Candice was born, Kristen emerged from jail a changed person.

Determined to be a good mother to her children, she began attending church, building her foundation in faith, and dedicating her life to her family.

"Three years later, the Lord led me back to the pregnancy crisis center and the ministry that had inspired me to keep my daughter," she said. Kristen served in the ministry for ten years.

In 2012, she founded "A Door of Hope," a faith-based nonprofit organization that helps girls thirteen years and older who are struggling with destructive behavioral patterns, addictions, sexual abuse, abortion issues, eating disorders, and depression. She started the organization in her home and soon relocated into the same building where she had once walked through the wrong door—the door that had changed her life. She began a prison ministry and started a women's retreat. She also wrote a book, *The Cry*, to help other young women with abortion-related trauma.

And while she motivated hundreds of young ladies to rebuild their lives, she also tried desperately to save her son, who had been battling his own addiction since he was a teenager. Ricky and Kristen had a warm, trusting relationship. Even when Ricky made mistakes, Kristen knew she could count on him to be honest with her. He had always been tenderhearted, a loving son and friend, a hard worker. He had a big smile that was mirrored in his striking blue eyes, but that smile masked an inner turmoil that he shared with no one.

Ricky, too, had experienced divine intervention several times. Once, Kristen was called to the hospital after he had been stabbed. Ricky survived. Another time, after a night of partying, he flipped his car and was ejected from the vehicle. He landed in a ravine. Again, he survived.

Then, on November 2, 2014, Ricky finally shared a terrible secret, one he had kept hidden for many years. "I was molested when I was little," he told his mother. Kristen was stunned.

"He was in pain. He was crying out for help. He had been numbing his pain with drugs and alcohol," she said. "Finally, I understood."

Kristen hugged him tightly, feeling his pain, hurting with him as only a mother can do. She tried to encourage him, to give him hope.

The next day, Ricky shot and killed himself in Kristen's bedroom closet. He was twenty-nine years old.

Kristen was devastated. "I blamed myself," she said. "I blamed my past. I thought if I had not been on drugs I would have known what had happened to him. I could barely get out of bed for months. I kept thinking, 'You can't help your own son, how can you help other people?' I simply couldn't function."

Realizing that Kristen was hitting rock bottom, the ladies at A Door of Hope held an intervention with her. "They encouraged me not to give up," she said. "I prayed and told God that I wanted something good to come out of Ricky's death."

Despite the overwhelming grief she felt, Kristen began suicide prevention training. She wanted to help people like Ricky, people who felt like there was no hope left. One day, a suicidal girl called in. Kristen answered the phone.

"It was a desperate situation," she said. "I prayed for God's guidance, and a miracle happened. I talked her through the crisis. One week later, she walked through our doors."

That was a turning point for Kristen. God had shown her that she could make a difference. She determined that she would live her life to serve as many people as she could. To date, Kristen has helped hundreds of young girls and women learn how to live a healthy, fulfilled life through Jesus Christ. A Door of Hope has also established the Ricky Maddox Jr. Never Lose Hope Scholarship in honor of her son.

Kristen's daughter Krisie became the first member of the family to graduate from college. She is now a wife, mother, and schoolteacher. Candice is currently attending college.

In an effort to reach more women, Kristen is writing another book, *Scars*, which chronicles the lives of five women who have broken the cycle of sexual abuse, domestic abuse, codependency, addiction, and obesity. She also publishes a magazine, *Voices of Hope.*

"By the grace of God, I made it through," Kristen said. "I now have a passion to encourage others like never before. I am living proof that God doesn't waste a single moment of our lives, even in our darkest days."

For more information, please visit www.adoorofhopela.com.

KARL GARCIA

Coping with the trauma of cancer

When Karl Garcia was in eighth grade, his mother, Sandra, was diagnosed with cancer, and Karl began drinking—"to cope with what was going on in my head," he said. Although he didn't understand exactly what that meant at the time, he knew it was serious. His parents had divorced when Karl was seven years old, and the young boy lived with his mother. Sandra was a kind, loving woman, a nurturer, and she did everything she could to give her son a good life. Then she was diagnosed, and suddenly every moment of his life became more urgent.

Karl spent the next three years helplessly watching his sweet mother fight for her life. He did everything he could for her, but her cancer was stronger than both of them. When Karl was sixteen, Sandra passed away.

Karl moved in with his father. "It was tough," he said. "I was just a kid, and I didn't know how to deal with such a great loss."

Karl used alcohol as a numbing device, but the pain didn't go away. He finished high school and enrolled in the University of Houston, where he earned a bachelor's degree in hotel and restaurant management. He still drank a lot—beer, wine, Crown Royal; it didn't really matter which—but nothing could soothe the emptiness he felt inside.

"I was quite the drinker," he said. "I drank anything to make myself feel better."

When he was twenty-one, Karl got married. He went to work for Houston's Restaurant, and during that time he became a father to three children. Karl's drinking escalated along with his stress level. He was arrested for driving under the influence of alcohol. He wrecked several cars. Karl knew things were getting out of control, and he was a man who needed to feel like he was in control.

One night, he went out drinking and realized he was in trouble. Around two o'clock in the morning, he called his father. "I can't stop," Karl told him. "I want to, but I can't."

The next morning, his father arranged for Karl to go to an outpatient treatment facility. "I went there every night for six months," Karl said. "I got sober, but drinking was only one part of my problem. I had this emptiness I couldn't shake. I was broken inside, and I didn't know how to fix me."

Karl couldn't fix his marriage, either, and soon divorced.

Wanting to give his children a better life, Karl partnered with some friends and opened a restaurant named Cavanaugh's in Clear Lake, Texas. The restaurant was successful, and he soon opened another and another. The pressure of business ownership began to take its toll.

"I always thought that everything depended on me," he said. "I put a lot of pressure on myself. I couldn't fail. I had to provide a good life for my children."

Karl became a sober, successful businessman who had everything he thought a man could want—wealth, women, respect—but he still wasn't happy. He simply went through the motions. "I was the guy who looked like he had it all together, but it was a façade. All the things I thought would bring me happiness didn't. I bounced along at rock bottom for many years."

In 1996, a friend suggested that Karl might enjoy volunteering at a children's hospital. Karl soon found himself pushing a book cart down the hospital's corridor, stopping in each room to give books to the children. Sometimes he played games with them. He read to them. He put puzzles together with them. He discovered that pushing that cart gave him tremendous satisfaction.

One day, he walked into a room and saw a pretty little girl sitting on the bed. "I'm Brooke," she said. "I'm two years old."

Karl smiled and introduced himself. Soon the two became fast friends, and Karl learned that Brooke had cancer. During one of his visits, Karl met her mother, Nichole Hawes. He identified with Nichole immediately. He knew what it was like to watch someone you love battle cancer. He and Nichole became friends and then began dating.

"We lost Brooke on New Year's Eve of the new millennium," Karl said. "It was such a difficult time for both of us. We were devastated. I didn't know how to help her, just as I had never been able to help myself."

Karl began searching for answers, trying to fill another hole in his heart. He kept reaching for God, but he didn't know who God was. He and Nichole began attending church together, a half dozen different ones before they landed at Clear Creek Community Church in League City, Texas.

"It was there I really heard the gospel for the first time, what God had done for me through Jesus. I learned how to trust God, to depend on Him. Through His gift, I was finally made whole," he said.

In 2005, Karl got out of the restaurant business, and the next year, he and Nichole married.

Before long, Karl went to work for a company that provides art to hospitals and other healthcare facilities. He had been there a couple of years when, one Monday while he was driving to work, he had the strangest thought: *You've spent your life building your kingdom. Now it's time to build Mine.*

Karl told Nichole about it. "I don't even think like that," he said. "I would never think the word, 'kingdom.'"

Karl called a friend and told him that he thought God had spoken to him.

The following Sunday, his senior pastor pulled him aside. "I'd like you to pray about something. I'd like you to leave your job and join our team."

Karl spent several months wrestling with the decision, although he already knew what God wanted him to do.

Today, Karl is the pastor at his church's Clear Lake Campus, where he ministers to approximately one thousand people each week. He provides oversight and uses the skills he learned as an entrepreneur to help his church community grow.

For most of his life, Karl had been trying to fill a void in his life. It only took a book cart and a little girl named Brooke to lead the way to happiness.

"I'm thankful every day for the new purpose and meaning in my life," he said. "Through Christ, I found ultimate peace and fulfillment."

For more information, please visit www.clearcreek.org.

MICHAEL "IRON MIKE" PETERSON

FROM SKID ROW TO THE WHEELHOUSE

At one time in his life, Michael "Iron Mike" Peterson could have been the poster child for the stereotypical skid row drunk—a bottle of cheap wine, wrapped in a brown paper bag, clutched in his hand as he staggered down the street looking for the next bench or alley where he could get a good night's sleep. For seventeen years, he lived on the street, sometimes finding a temporary home in a beer joint, occasionally sleeping on a friend's couch, but mostly curling up under a thin blanket in some back alley, hoping for a few hours of rest.

Iron Mike had been homeless since he was thirteen years old. When he was seventeen, he was sent to prison in Texas for stealing building materials from a construction site. Upon his release at the age of twenty, he had nowhere to go but back to the street. Wine became the only comfort he knew—his warmth on a cold night, his retreat from the world. Some of those years are now a blur, distant memories buried beneath the weight of shame and low self-esteem.

"I went in and out of detox facilities many times, but nothing worked," Iron Mike said.

In October 1989, Iron Mike entered The Wheelhouse and sobered up for ten months. For the first time, he had hope of leading a normal life, but then he picked up the bottle again. He returned to The Wheelhouse in March 1991, and this time he stayed sober for two and a half years. As happens with many recovering alcoholics, Iron Mike succumbed to temptation and returned to his old habits. In January 1994, he made his way back to The Wheelhouse, and he has not had a drink since.

"The Wheelhouse helped save my life and gave me the foundation I needed to stay sober and become a respected citizen. Alcoholics Anonymous (AA) and the Twelve Steps gave me a different life," he said.

When he left The Wheelhouse, Iron Mike got a job working turnarounds and maintenance in plants in the Houston area. He rented a house in Bacliff, Texas. "At the age of thirty-seven, I paid my first electric bill," he said. "That was the first time I had ever had a home."

Even as he rebuilt his own life, Iron Mike realized that the way to total fulfillment was to share his message of hope with other men like him. He became a volunteer at The Wheelhouse and soon discovered that giving of himself to other alcoholics gave his own life more meaning and helped him stay the course. He continues to serve as an active member of The Wheelhouse's board of directors.

In 2006, he started his own business, Iron Mike's Motorcycle Shop, which services and sometimes builds motorcycles. Nine years ago, he founded The

Wheelhouse Motorcycle Rally, which features The Wheelhouse Monument Run, a seventy-mile escorted road trip held the first weekend of October. "We raise about $60,000 for The Wheelhouse each year," Iron Mike said. "We hold a raffle for a motorcycle and have live bands. It's a lot of fun for a great cause."

Today, Iron Mike is grateful for so many things in life—his warm bed; the home he rented so many years ago that he now owns; his wife, Gloria, whom he married in 2014; his daughter, Sarah, with whom he reunited after nineteen years; and The Wheelhouse, which helped him find his way to sobriety.

"The Wheelhouse gave me a second chance at life," he said. "I have watched thousands go through the House, and many are just like me. They stay sober, get their families back, gain employment, and become respected members of their churches and communities. Until the day I die, I will have a great appreciation for The Wheelhouse and AA. These organizations gave me dignity and taught me how to a live meaningful life."

For more information, please visit www.thewheelhouseinc.com or www.aa.org.

THERESA WESTBROOK

TALK SHOW HOST BREAKS SILENCE ON ABUSE

One of seven children, Theresa Westbrook grew up in the North Texas area during an era when no one talked about child molestation. That was a dirty secret usually swept under the rug. Theresa and her siblings lived in poverty, partially due to the fact that her father was an alcoholic. In her home, no one but Theresa knew what happened on those nights when her father got drunk and snuck into her bedroom while she was sleeping.

Theresa's earliest childhood memories are her father's breath on her face and his offending hands. The abuse began at the age of four and continued until she was thirteen years old. At first, she didn't understand what was happening to her. She simply thought that was her father's way of showing affection. By the age of ten, she realized that something was very wrong, but from the first assault, her father had warned her not to tell anyone, threatening her with the fact that Daddy would go to jail or her mother would leave and split up the family. She loved her family and wanted to remain with her siblings, so Theresa kept quiet. She coped with the abuse the only way she knew how at that tender age—by pretending to sleep through it.

"One time, my mother separated from him, and I begged her not to go back," Theresa said. "She didn't understand why I did not want her to reunite with my father, but I couldn't tell her. I was afraid it would destroy my family if I shared my secret." The family reunited, and the abuse continued.

When Theresa was thirteen, her mother divorced her father. Theresa finally summoned the courage to tell her mother what had happened to her since she was a child. "She was so upset," Theresa remembered, "but he moved away, and I didn't have to see him anymore."

Throughout her childhood, Theresa attended church with her grandmother during family visits. Theresa's faith in the redeeming sacrifice of Christ grew strong, and she listened carefully to the sermons about God's love and forgiveness. "The spirit of God gave me compassion and mercy to forgive my father. We seldom spoke, but during any written or verbal communications, I would always tell him that God would forgive him of all of his sins," she said. "I told him all he needed to do was to ask God for forgiveness."

For many years, Theresa's mother and then later Theresa's husband, Don Westbrook, were the only people who knew she had been sexually abused, although Theresa did not share the details with them. "I suffered so many complex emotions," she explained. "I felt like I was buried under a pile of life-crushing rocks. I was confused and ashamed. Even though I forgave my father, I had leftover anger and resentment. I suffered from low self-esteem, anxiety, and depression. I was broken inside."

On the outside, Theresa was warm, friendly, outgoing. She became a nurse and an ordained minister and dedicated her life to caring for others. For years, though, Theresa felt weighted down by the pain of her past. She suffered silently, praying that God would help her find her way to understanding, peace, and restoration.

In 2008, Theresa felt divinely inspired to write her story, *A Strand of Pearls*, in an effort to help victims of childhood sexual abuse. Through the process of writing and editing, she shared her story with her editor. It was the first time she had talked about it with anyone other than her mother and her husband. "It was liberating to finally talk about the abuse in detail and share all I had learned through this tragedy," she said. "I wanted readers to understand the pain childhood sexual abuse causes, but more importantly, I wanted them to know the depth of healing and restoration I found through Jesus Christ."

Theresa and Don, who is also a minister, cofounded Pearls of Shalom Ministries, a nonprofit organization that reaches out to help those who have suffered from childhood sexual abuse. Theresa also wrote a follow-up book, *The Advocates of the Abused and Silent*, giving a voice to other childhood sexual abuse victims she has encountered. She donates her books to family crisis agencies, chaplains, correctional institutions, ministries, and survivors, and to counselors who treat both victims and sex offenders.

"My goal is to offer hope and healing to victims and accountability and hope for change to sexual abusers," she said. "Incest is one of the deepest wounds a child can suffer emotionally. It is very confusing and can promote a lifetime of negative results. I encourage victims to get faith-based counseling because there truly is a greater life waiting for you through Christ."

Theresa also serves in faith-affirming media organizations and produces *Time with Theresa*, a popular television talk show, which airs in Denton, Texas, and features inspirational guests, unsung heroes, and a variety of stories designed to enlighten, inspire, and entertain the public.

For more information, please visit www.theresawestbrook.com.

JEREMIAH FRY

CRACKED OUT TO CHRISTLIKE

Jeremiah Fry struggled with insecurity for much of his life. He was raised in Littleton, Colorado, approximately thirty miles south of Denver. His parents, Elizabeth and Jonathan Fry, married when Elizabeth discovered she was pregnant. When Jeremiah was three, his brother Josh was born. Elizabeth and Jonathan were loving parents to their children, but they both struggled with alcoholism. They soon divorced, and Jeremiah and Josh rotated back and forth between their parents' homes. Jeremiah was raised on Christian principles, but he had no real role models in his life.

Jonathan remarried when Jeremiah was six. Before long, the young boy had two more brothers Jacob and Jonah. "I loved my brothers, but I felt like everything in my father's house was about them," Jeremiah said. "I was a child struggling to cope with a rapidly changing family dynamic."

When Jeremiah was a teenager, a technique used for braces caused a large gap between his front teeth. He became afraid to open his mouth or let anyone see him eat. He sat alone during lunch each day, isolating himself from his classmates.

In his junior year, Jeremiah decided to pursue his dream of becoming an actor. He took an acting class and earned a role in the school's production of *Grease*. He began making new friends, thespians who liked to drink and smoke weed. Jeremiah, craving acceptance, indulged with them. Soon his braces came off, and he gained a small measure of confidence.

After he graduated, Jeremiah began waiting tables at a restaurant. One night, some friends from the restaurant asked him to go to a party. Jeremiah was already so drunk that he could barely walk, but he tagged along. That night, he was introduced to cocaine.

"Through coke, I became the life of the party," he said. "It gave me a false sense of confidence—powder confidence. I was soon more addicted to the person I became on coke than to the actual drug."

Over time, Jeremiah's addiction grew, and he lost his job. With no money and an expensive habit, he turned to selling drugs. "I became a meth head and began selling coke and weed to support my habit," he said.

And then he tried crack. Soon nothing else mattered. Even through the fog of drugs, Jeremiah realized how fast he was going down. He reached out to his uncle, who was a pastor in San Diego, for help and then moved there determined to change his life. His determination didn't last. One hit off a joint in a moment of weakness, and he was gone again.

"I thought about killing myself," Jeremiah said. "I realized I had failed at everything in my life, so I knew I wouldn't be successful at suicide either. Ironically, that realization kept me alive."

Jeremiah decided to move to Los Angeles, where he could be closer to his mother and his brother Josh, and where he could chase his dream of becoming an actor. He found an agent and got a few small roles, but he could not curtail his drug use, even for his dream.

Deflated and feeling more unworthy than ever, Jeremiah moved back to Colorado. Early one morning soon after he returned, he was standing outside of his car smoking a rock of crack when he hit the pavement. He regained consciousness a few minutes later and saw blood running down his gravel-pitted arms. He stood up and looked into the rearview mirror. His face looked just like his arms—bloody and pitted from drug use. Staring at the evidence of what his life had become, Jeremiah hit rock bottom. He cried out, "Lord, please help me."

A few weeks later, he entered Teen Challenge, a faith-based rehabilitation facility in New Orleans. On his first night there, August 20, 2004, the lights went off at 10:00 p.m. Jeremiah lay in his unfamiliar bed for a few minutes and then turned over and got on his knees. He began praying: "Lord, I'm Yours. I want to live my life for You."

Jeremiah meant what he said. Even the infamous French Quarter couldn't sway his resolve. Whenever he went there to witness, he had a Bible in his hand.

After he successfully completed the first phase of the program, Jeremiah was sent to the small town of Winnfield, located in north Louisiana, for the second phase. He began working in a thrift store run by Teen Challenge, and it was there that he met Ashley. The date is forever etched in their minds. It was the same day Hurricane Katrina destroyed the homes of everyone in Ashley's family.

For Jeremiah, it was love at first sight, but Ashley needed some persuading. Jeremiah won over her family, and they convinced Ashley to go out on a date with him.

Jeremiah completed the program, and he and Ashley married in November 2006.

The couple soon began attending Church of the King in Mandeville, Louisiana. It was there that Jeremiah was given the opportunity to live his dream. He was hired to help with video production at the church. A few years later, he opened his own video production company as a side business just as Louisiana was becoming a hotspot for the movie-making industry. Suddenly, he found himself working in production on major motion pictures.

On August 20, 2012, Ashley and Jeremiah welcomed their daughter, Maleah, into the world. "My daughter was born at 10:13 p.m., at the exact moment I gave my life to Christ eight years before. I know that was God's way of telling me He loved me," Jeremiah said.

Two years later, their son, Judah, was born.

Although Jeremiah had turned his life around, he still struggled with insecurity now and then. One day, while studying the Bible, he had a revelation. He was reading Psalm 139:16: "Your eyes saw my substance, being yet unformed. And in Your book they were all written, the days fashioned for me, when as yet there were none of them."

"I realized that I had always felt like I was a mistake because my mom got pregnant when she was so young. That had haunted me my whole life," he said. "As I read that verse, it became clear that I wasn't a mistake, that God had already mapped out my life before I was born."

The desperate need to be accepted and the lingering thoughts that he didn't belong disappeared. He was no longer the hurting young man who had fallen to the pavement strung out on crack. He now felt secure in the knowledge that his life had purpose.

Jeremiah soon had another revelation. He realized that the Lord wanted more from him. Everything he had worked on in the past had entertainment value—*Terminator Genisys*, *Jack Reacher: Never Go Back*, *Max*, *The Best of Me*, *Pitch Perfect 2*, and *Deepwater Horizon*—but none of his work had what he calls "kingdom" value. He began producing and directing documentaries, videos, films, and commercials that provide inspiration and hope. He now wants his work to touch people spiritually and emotionally. The passion he once had for acting has evolved into a passion for creating productions that have the power to change lives.

"I've been blessed," Jeremiah said. "The devil said 'addict,' but God said 'apostle.' The devil said 'pothead,' but God said 'prophet.' The devil said 'cracked out,' but God said 'Christlike.' When I finally reached out to Him, God gave my life purpose. Now it's my turn to give."

For more information, please visit www.teenchallengeusa.com or www.limfilms.com.

KEN PAXTON

WOMEN, WHISKEY, AND BEER—A COMPLETE TURNAROUND

"**P**repare yourselves. I don't think he's going to make it," the neurosurgeon said to Ken Paxton's parents. The seven-year-old lay on a gurney being prepped for surgery, only four inches of scalp covering his head—his injury the result of a lawnmower accident.

"You may be rolling your sleeves down, but the good Lord is rolling His up," Ken's father responded, and he began to pray for a miracle. Ken's parents were Christians, and their faith was strong.

They got their miracle. Ken survived the surgery and soon recovered, but there were some things he couldn't do. In school, he wanted to participate in sports, but the accident held him back.

As Ken grew older, he became frustrated by his limitations, and he suffered from low self-esteem. When he was in sixth grade, his parents divorced, and his feelings of frustration escalated.

In high school, Ken discovered that writing could provide an outlet for his emotions. He began to vent on paper, giving himself some small measure of therapy. After he graduated, Ken attended Northeast Louisiana University (now the University of Louisiana at Monroe), where he studied to become an athletic trainer. Although he enjoyed his classes, Ken soon realized this wasn't the career path for him. He quit school and, soon after, he married his first wife, whose father was an instrument technician. Ken enjoyed listening to his father-in-law's stories about his job, and he decided he wanted to be an instrument technician, as well. He soon found employment working turnarounds in the oil industry.

Although his marriage lasted only two years, Ken was grateful that he had found a career he loved. After his divorce, he focused on rebuilding his life, living for the Lord, and looking forward to a bright future.

Two years later, he married again—a marriage that would last eight years and give him his son, Kyland. When he divorced for the second time, Ken began venting his frustrations in a new way.

"I started associating with the wrong crowd," he said. "On the weekends that I didn't have my son, I drank. I went to bars and strip clubs. I began hanging out with local bands and partying real hard—chasing women and drinking beer, vodka, whiskey. I turned away from God."

This was against everything his parents had taught him. Ken had been raised in the church. He had always tried to live a good life, but everything had become overwhelming after his second divorce.

"I was trying to find peace, and I used alcohol as an escape," he said. "I talked with my father about my problem, and he told me that this wasn't the way I was supposed to live. I knew he was right, but I couldn't stop."

Finally a friend, Jeff Gaudet, confronted Ken. "Why are you living this way after God has done so much for you?" Jeff asked. "What are you doing? I'm coming over to get you, and if I have to put you in a headlock, I'm bringing you back to church."

Jeff was true to his word. He brought Ken to a Christian conference for men, and Ken rededicated his life to Christ.

Soon after, Ken met Brandi Babin, who would become his third wife and the love of his life. Brandi also became his biggest champion. Ken had started writing a book during his second marriage, but he had never finished it. When he told Brandi about it, she insisted that he complete it and then helped him get the book published. Today, Ken uses his book, *Are You in Need of a Turnaround? A 21-Day Devotional for Men,* as a tool to help men who are struggling in their lives.

Ken also speaks at men's conferences and seminars, encouraging participants to seek transformation through the Lord. "So many men need to have a turnaround in their life; they need to get back on track," he said. "I've been there. I'm living proof that miracles happen. Through sharing my story about God's grace and mercy, I encourage others to put their lives in God's hands. He will do the rest."

For more information, please visit www.aa.org.

MINDY CRANE

Stripper saved by a dream

Mindy Crane grew up in New Orleans with twelve siblings—two biological, seven half, and three step. Her father, Robert, had met her mother, Nilamenta, in Pago Pago, the capital of American Samoa on the island of Tutuila. Robert, who was in the Navy, brought Nilamenta to the United States, and the two were married.

Mindy was two years old when Nilamenta informed Robert that her sister had passed away and that she needed to return home. Robert bought her a round-trip ticket, and Nilamenta flew to Pago Pago. When Nilamenta's sister showed up at their home that Christmas, alive and well, Robert knew his wife was not coming back. Mindy never saw her mother again.

Robert soon remarried, and Mindy and her two sisters were left alone with their stepmother and step-siblings while Robert worked offshore. Mindy had difficulty transitioning into her new, much larger family.

Mindy's younger sister, who had heart problems, was sent to her grandmother's home. Her older sister ran away and was eventually placed in a group home. Without her sisters, Mindy felt very alone and afraid. Beginning at the age of eleven, she attempted suicide at least once each year. When she was sixteen, she ran away.

Soon a friend gave Mindy the option of going to work for an escort service or getting a job at a notorious gentlemen's club in New Orleans East. Mindy thought the strip club would be the lesser of two evils, and using her stepsister's identification, she applied for the job.

"The first night, I was scared to death," she said. "I was just standing there, hugging the pole. A guy got on the microphone and said, 'This is a strip club. Take off your clothes.' I took off my clothes, but I was so embarrassed."

Mindy's stage persona, Pocahontas, earned the young girl a lot of money—sometimes $1,000 per night or more. Mindy enjoyed the money she made, but she didn't like being groped and fondled by strangers who threw dollar bills at her. She began using drugs—ecstasy, acid, cocaine, Valium—anything to help her cope with her new reality.

"At sixteen, I worked six or seven nights every week," she said. "There's so much that goes on in those kinds of clubs. Sometimes a bus would pull up filled with rich men in business suits, and they could pick which girl they wanted. I saw things at sixteen that no girl should see."

One night, Mindy went out with a group of friends, and someone slipped GHB (otherwise known as "the date rape drug") into her drink. Mindy was raped that night. It would not be the last time. "Every time I got raped, I felt like it was my fault because of the dangerous lifestyle I was living," she said.

When she was seventeen, Mindy became pregnant. She stopped stripping for a while and tried to live a better life. Mindy's boyfriend left her after her son, Jacob, was born, and she soon found that the kinds of jobs she could get didn't pay the bills.

She returned to stripping. For the next few years, Mindy moved from one club to the next, sometimes getting fired for snorting lines of coke at work, other times quitting when she was no longer able to deal with management's demands. The young girl who had once felt so vulnerable and afraid had been hardened by drug addiction and conditioned to depravity by the amount of money she made.

In 2001, Mindy got married and began partying more than ever. She and her husband threw lavish parties that sometimes lasted a week, and crystal meth became her drug of choice. Her second child, Khalia, was born when she was twenty-six. By this time, Mindy was in so deep that she felt like there was no way back to a good life. She had no bar by which to measure what a good life meant. All she had ever known was dysfunction.

"A friend of mine started attending Bible study, and he would tell me what he had learned," she said. "I listened carefully to everything he said, and I prayed that God would help me get out. Sometimes things have to get a lot worse before we listen to what God is telling us."

Things came to a head when Mindy was promoted to the position of events coordinator. Part of her job included planning special events for the other strippers. "I drove a promotional vehicle with half-naked girls plastered all over it," she said. "When I became part of exploiting these girls, I couldn't live with myself. I started having seizures on the way to every event."

In 2008, after attending a luau she had coordinated, Mindy overdosed. "I wouldn't wake up," she said. "I knew I had pushed too far because I could feel my spirit being stripped away from my body."

Mindy felt like she was traveling through a tunnel. "The further up I went, the more I began to feel like I was surrounded with this feeling of love and joy. My questions were being answered before I asked them. I saw Peter and Paul talking, and I said, 'Oh, the Bible's real.' They said, 'You better believe it. Why aren't you at home with your kids?' I thought about my children, and I got so scared, but then I could feel God's love surrounding me. He said, 'Don't you know you're a mother?' Then I had the strangest vision. It was like I saw the whole universe coming together into the shape of a cross. Beautiful voices were singing, 'For the Bible tells me so.' I woke up completely sober."

Mindy went home and told her husband what had happened. Determined to change her life, Mindy and Pocahontas retired from stripping at the age of thirty. Mindy began attending church and reading the Bible.

Two years later, she welcomed another child, Sophia, into her family.

"God transformed my life and my husband's life," she said. "I did a lot of soul-searching for a few years. I had a hunger for the truth, and I learned everything I could about how to live a godly life."

Before long, Mindy began reaching out to the homeless in her area. "There are so many homeless people where I live. I buy them food, socks, whatever I can afford to help make their lives better," she said. "I also help them contact family members. Today, we have a group of people who work together to feed and witness to the homeless."

In 2015, Mindy started her own ministry. Every Friday night, she hosts worship services and invites those whom she knows need God the most. She ministers to women at the rehab facility where she was treated. She facilitates prayer teams and has a phone ministry. She also counsels women struggling with addiction.

"I'm not an ordained minister, but I feel like I've been ordained by the Lord," she said. "I never thought life could be this awesome, but when I was at death's door, God showed me the way to happiness."

For more information about Mindy's ministry, please call (504) 539-0642.

BRADLEY BLUE

RELIVING THE HORRORS OF WAR—PTSD

On August 2, 1990, Saddam Hussein's Republican Guard invaded Kuwait. Neighboring Arab countries called upon the United Nations Security Council and the United States to stop the invasion. One of the largest coalitions of countries from around the world formed an alliance, and Operation Desert Storm commenced January 17, 1991, in the form of air strikes.

Bradley Blue, an Army tank commander known as "Blue," sat in his living room in Spring, Texas, in October 1990, watching the drama unfold. On leave from his post in Aschaffenburg, Germany, he searched the news for any signs that his unit had been deployed to the Middle East. When his leave was over, he flew to Germany, expecting to return to his normal routine. Two days later, he found himself on a plane headed for Saudi Arabia.

Blue's unit was moved to assembly areas until it was time to push in through Central Iraq. On February 23, the ground war began.

"We engaged the Republican Guard and took twenty thousand prisoners," Blue said. "When the battle was over, we set up a checkpoint on Highway 8, where we searched vehicles and processed prisoners."

It was some of those prisoners who would later trigger Blue's nightmares. "Collateral damage," it's commonly called—the men, women, and children who get caught in the crossfire of war. Blue stared at the children, some missing arms or legs, others whose faces had been burned and cut by shrapnel, still others whose bodies were wrapped in blood-soaked gauze.

"It was horrifying to see those children. I had to wonder if the artillery from my tank had caused this. You know people will get hurt in a war, but it's not real to you. You have a job to do, and you do it. But seeing something like this—man, it's tough."

Blue had joined the Army soon after he quit high school, just two weeks before graduation. In November 1982, he reported to basic training. The eager young soldier began his career as a cavalry scout and completed his training at Fort Knox Armor School.

After basic training, Blue returned to Texas to marry his high school sweetheart, Crystle. In 1984, he was deployed to the Republic of Korea.

"I got introduced to Lady Death in Korea," Blue said. "At twenty-one, I was seeing and experiencing things I could not have imagined before."

While in Korea, Blue's son, Bradley Steven Blue Jr., was born, but it would be eight months before Blue saw his baby boy in person. In late 1986, Blue left Korea and headed for his new post at Fort Polk in Louisiana. His daughter, Brittany Lynn, was born in June 1987.

In 1988, the family moved to Germany, where Blue continued in his role as a tank commander. Six months later, Crystle and the children returned stateside when Crystle learned that her father had cancer.

Blue exited the service September 3, 1993.

By July 1994, he was divorced. Without taking the time to address the issues that had caused the breakup of his marriage, he fell in love again. He married his second wife, Sherri, that September.

"I knew something was wrong with me," Blue said. "I was having a hard time, having nightmares, but I didn't tell anyone about them. I couldn't. I was trying so hard to appear normal, and I began drinking more and more."

Before long, Jack Daniel's and Blue became best friends. "When I was in the military, I would have two drinks before bed," he said. "During my second marriage, two drinks became my first and last, with a whole lot in between."

By July 1999, Blue was divorced again.

The next year he married his third wife, Deborah, and the couple had a daughter, Misty Skye Blue.

Blue's nightmares became more and more frequent. Most nights, he lay in bed, staring in the darkness at the ceiling. He was afraid to close his eyes. He knew what would be waiting there. It was always the same—the children, their bodies mangled, their limbs obliterated. Their faces morphing into the faces of his own children.

Or there would be a fire, an explosion in his tank. He was trapped inside—burning, his skin melting away as the flames engulfed him.

"I isolated myself from everyone, my friends, my family," Blue said. "I drank all the time. Deborah hung in there with me as long as she could."

In 2011, Deborah asked Blue to leave.

For the next three years, he stumbled through life—working different jobs, drinking to numb the pain, suffering from the same nightmares that had plagued him since the day he saw those children. He had no idea that he was suffering from post-traumatic stress disorder (PTSD).

"On August 12, 2014, I hit rock bottom," Blue said. "I was tired. Tired of life. Tired of the nightmares. I was a disgrace, an embarrassment. No one in my family wanted to talk to me."

After finishing off a bottle of vodka, he pulled out his pistol. He was staring at it contemplating his death when he heard a voice on the radio. "If you are a veteran looking to hurt yourself, call this number," the voice said.

"I thought I was hearing things, but then it repeated," Blue said. "I called the number and told the guy who answered, 'You're full of crap.' Then I hung up."

Ten seconds later, Blue's phone rang. He didn't answer, but Alex Vitek left a message: "Someone does care. You are not alone."

It was enough to make Blue put down his gun.

The next morning, he decided to check out the place the guy on the radio had mentioned—Camp Hope. He figured if he got there by 9:30 a.m., he could hit the liquor store on his way back. Blue sat in the parking lot wondering if he was going to summon up the courage to get out of his vehicle.

Finally, Alex walked over to his car. "He asked me the most important question I've ever been asked in my life," Blue said. "'Do you need some help?' My journey to recovery started at that moment."

Blue spent eight months at Camp Hope in Houston. Through talking about his problems, Blue learned how to cope with the anger and guilt that had plagued him for so long.

"I had never heard of PTSD, but then I'd been swimming in a bottle for twenty-four years," Blue said. "I discovered that others had the same story I had, only different names and different dates."

While at Camp Hope, Blue realized he needed to make amends with his family. He invited Deborah to visit him. For the first time, he told her what he had experienced. "She's now a part of my support group and a true blessing in my life," he said.

Deborah and Blue said their recommitment vows soon after.

In July 2015, Blue accepted an offer to become a veterans coordinator at Camp Hope. He spent the next eight months mentoring other veterans with PTSD, but then he began to feel their pain too intensely. Blue's counselor recommended that he take a sabbatical. "Because of Camp Hope, I now recognize when I need to work on me," he said.

Blue's best advice to other combat veterans is, "No matter what you think, there is always hope. You can be anything you want to be. Just ask for help because help and hope are available."

For more information about Camp Hope, please visit www.ptsdusa.org or call (832) 912-4429.

EPILOGUE

As we have learned from the stories of the people we've featured, hitting rock bottom is never easy. Rock bottom is usually many years in the making and the result of our reactions to the circumstances of our lives. For most people, hitting rock bottom can be freeing because there is only one direction we can go from there—up.

When we reach the lowest point in our lives, we are forced to reassess our choices. We learn that our way of doing things will simply no longer work. At rock bottom, our secrets are revealed, our flaws are exposed, and all the reasons for lying to ourselves and to those in our lives disappear. This can be very liberating, enabling us to finally move forward in truth.

At rock bottom, we are forced to seek help for our emotional problems and our addictions, which leads to understanding about the triggers that cause us to behave so erratically. We are given the tools we need to address our issues. Through understanding, we learn how to regain control of our lives. Hitting bottom forces us to face the facts, to realize that we have to change, and to make adjustments that lead to new opportunities for growth.

We also learn to take responsibility for our actions, perhaps for the first time, and with that responsibility comes forgiveness, humility, and compassion. At the bottom, we can finally learn to trust ourselves, which leads us to a new level of respect for ourselves and for others. We gain a new sense of self, of purpose, and we can then use our experiences to help others like us.

By the time we hit rock bottom, most of us have realized that there are no guarantees in life. Family members and friends, weary from the late night phone calls, have long passed the point where they are willing to help. We must now rely on ourselves. Through experiencing the darkest moments possible, we learn to be grateful for the simplest things—food, clothes, shelter, a kind word, a caring heart. Survival is no small thing. We can now look at ourselves in the mirror and feel proud. We've been to the bottom, and we've survived.

We have come back wiser, better, stronger.

And when we use the lessons we learned on our way to the bottom, we can help others to turn their lives around, as well.

Other times, rock bottom is forced upon us through tragedies beyond our control—the death of a loved one, a debilitating injury, horrors we witness. When we experience unimaginable events, grief and trauma can cause us to spiral downward. When the rug is pulled from under us, depression can destabilize our normal decision-making processes, and we sometimes react in ways that are harmful to our well-being. Our inability to cope with loss or trauma can result in suicidal feelings or create a dependence on alcohol or drugs. It is important during these times to recognize the power these emotions have over us.

If you feel that everything in your life is spinning out of control, if you are drowning in grief, if you are plagued by addictions, or if you need help coping with any problem you may have, we urge you to reach out for help. Seek a counselor, a minister, an organization, anyone who can help you on your way to recovery. If the first thing you try doesn't work, try and try again until you are successful. Do not give up on yourself. Know that you are worth the effort.

When we are down and out, faith and hope have incredible powers to lead us back to productive lives. Nurture your spirituality as you nurture your mind and body. Become proactive in your own recovery using faith and hope as your cornerstones.

Finally, it is important to remember that this is not all about you. It's about those who helped you find your way back to a happy life. Now it's your turn to give. You may be surprised to discover that when you focus on others, your life becomes more meaningful and your resolve becomes stronger.

Reach out your hand and pull someone else at rock bottom back with you.

SELF-ASSESSMENTS

Alcoholics Anonymous poses the following questions to help you determine if you may be an alcoholic. If you answer "yes" to any of the following questions, please reach out for help by visiting www.aa.org.

1. Have I tried to stop drinking for a week or so but could not do it?

2. Have I wished people would stop talking about my drinking?

3. Have I changed drinks to try not to get drunk?

4. Do I ever need a drink to get going in the morning?

5. Do I envy people who can drink without getting into trouble?

6. Does my drinking cause problems at home?

7. Does my drinking cause problems with other people?

8. Do I try to get extra drinks?

9. Have I tried to stop drinking but still got drunk?

10. Have I missed work or cut school because of drinking?

11. Do I have blackouts—times I cannot remember?

12. Would my life be better if I quit drinking?

Because Alcoholics Anonymous has helped so many people overcome their addictions, we felt it was important to include the Twelve Steps and the Twelve Traditions, as well as a brief excerpt from the fourth edition of the *Big Book*, which are core principles of the organization. To read a complete version of the *Big Book*, please visit www.aa.org.

The Twelve Steps:

1. We admitted we were powerless over alcohol—that our lives had become unmanageable.

2. Came to believe that a Power greater than ourselves could restore us to sanity.

3. Made a decision to turn our will and our lives over to the care of God as we understood Him.

4. Made a searching and fearless moral inventory of ourselves.

5. Admitted to God, to ourselves, and to another human being the exact nature of our wrongs.

6. Were entirely ready to have God remove all these defects of character.

7. Humbly asked Him to remove our shortcomings.

8. Made a list of all persons we had harmed, and became willing to make amends to them all.

9. Made direct amends to such people wherever possible, except when to do so would injure them or others.

10. Continued to take personal inventory and when we were wrong promptly admitted it.

11. Sought through prayer and meditation to improve our conscious contact with God, as we understood Him, praying only for knowledge of His will for us and the power to carry that out.

12. Having had a spiritual awakening as the result of these Steps, we tried to carry this message to alcoholics, and to practice these principles in all our affairs.

Excerpt from pages 83 and 84 of the *Big Book*:

If we are painstaking about this phase of our development, we will be amazed before we are half way through. We are going to know a new freedom and a new happiness. We will not regret the past nor wish to shut the door on it. We will comprehend the word serenity and we will know peace. No matter how far down the scale we have gone, we will see how our experience can benefit others. That feeling of uselessness and self-pity will disappear. We will lose interest in selfish things and gain interest in our fellows. Self-seeking will slip away. Our whole attitude and outlook upon life will change. Fear of people and of economic insecurity will leave us. We will intuitively know how to handle situations which used to baffle us. We will suddenly realize that God is doing for us what we could not do for ourselves.

Are these extravagant promises? We think not. They are being fulfilled among us—sometimes quickly, sometimes slowly. They will always materialize if we work for them.

The Twelve Traditions:

1. Our common welfare should come first; personal recovery depends upon A.A. unity.

2. For our group purpose there is but one ultimate authority—a loving God as He may express Himself in our group conscience. Our leaders are but trusted servants; they do not govern.

3. The only requirement for A.A. membership is a desire to stop drinking.

4. Each group should be autonomous except in matters affecting other groups or A.A.as a whole.

5. Each group has but one primary purpose—to carry its message to the alcoholic who still suffers.

6. An A.A. group ought never endorse, finance or lend the A.A. name to any related facility or outside enterprise, lest problems of money, property and prestige divert us from our primary purpose.

7. Every A.A. group ought to be fully self-supporting, declining outside contributions.

8. Alcoholics Anonymous should remain forever nonprofessional, but our service centers may employ special workers.

9. A.A., as such, ought never be organized; but we may create service boards or committees directly responsible to those they serve.

10. Alcoholics Anonymous has no opinion on outside issues; hence the A.A. name ought never be drawn into public controversy.

11. Our public relations policy is based on attraction rather than promotion; we need always maintain personal anonymity at the level of press, radio and films.

12. Anonymity is the spiritual foundation of all our Traditions, ever reminding us to place principles before personalities.

The Twelve Steps and the Twelve Traditions are reprinted with permission of Alcoholics Anonymous World Services, Inc. ("A.A.W.S.") Permission to reprint the Twelve Steps and the Twelve Traditions does not mean that A.A.W.S. has reviewed or approved the contents of this publication, or that A.A. necessarily agrees with the views expressed herein. A.A. is a program of recovery from alcoholism only—use of the Twelve Steps and Twelve Traditions in connection with programs and activities which are patterned after A.A., but which address other problems, or in any other non-A.A., does not imply otherwise.

The National Council on Alcoholism and Drug Dependence developed the following self-test for the purpose of determining drug addiction. If you need help, please visit www.ncadd.org for a list of resources in your area.

1. Have you used drugs other than those required for medicinal reasons?

2. Have you used prescription drugs at higher doses than recommended or needed to obtain a new prescription before the due date?

3. Do you use more than one drug at a time?

4. Can you get through the week without using drugs?

5. Are you always able to stop using drugs when you want to?

6. Have you had blackouts or flashbacks as a result of drug use?

7. Do you ever feel bad or guilty about your drug use?

8. Does your spouse (or parents) ever complain about your involvement with drugs?

9. Has drug use created problems between you and your spouse or your parents?

10. Have you lost friends because of your use of drugs?

11. Have you neglected your family because of your use of drugs?

12. Have you been in trouble at work because of drug use?

13. Have you lost a job because of drug use?

14. Have you gotten into fights when under the influence of drugs?

15. Have you engaged in illegal activities in order to obtain drugs?

16. Have you been arrested for possession of illegal drugs?

17. Have you ever experienced withdrawal symptoms (felt sick) when you stopped taking drugs?

18. Have you had medical problems as a result of your drug use (e.g. memory loss, hepatitis, convulsions, bleeding, etc.)?

19. Have you gone to anyone for help for a drug problem?

20. Have you been involved in a treatment program specifically related to drug use?

Gamblers Anonymous suggests you take the following test if you feel you may have a problem with compulsive gambling. To learn about resources to combat this addiction, please visit www.gamblersanonymous.org or www.lanieshope.org.

1. Did you ever lose time from work or school due to gambling?

2. Has gambling ever made your home life unhappy?

3. Did gambling affect your reputation?

4. Have you ever felt remorse after gambling?

5. Did you ever gamble to get money with which to pay debts or otherwise solve financial difficulties?

6. Did gambling cause a decrease in your ambition or efficiency?

7. After losing, did you feel you must return as soon as possible and win back your losses?

8. After a win, did you have a strong urge to return and win more?

9. Did you often gamble until your last dollar was gone?

10. Did you ever borrow to finance your gambling?

11. Have you ever sold anything to finance gambling?

12. Were you reluctant to use "gambling money" for normal expenditures?

13. Did gambling make you careless of the welfare of yourself or your family?

14. Did you ever gamble longer than you had planned?

15. Have you ever gambled to escape worry, trouble, boredom, loneliness, grief, or loss?

16. Have you ever committed, or considered committing, an illegal act to finance gambling?

17. Did gambling cause you to have difficulty in sleeping?

18. Do arguments, disappointments, or frustrations create within you an urge to gamble?

19. Did you ever have an urge to celebrate any good fortune by a few hours of gambling?

20. Have you ever considered self-destruction or suicide as a result of your gambling?

The following test can help you determine if you are a sex addict. If you answer "yes" to multiple questions, you may need to seek professional help. Resources are available at www.faithfulandtrue.com.

1. Do you engage in risky sexual behavior without regard to consequences?

2. Do you have sex with multiple partners at the same time?

3. Do you feel guilt or shame about the number of sexual partners you have?

4. Do you want to stop your sexual behavior, but can't?

5. Do you engage in pornography and masturbation multiple times per day?

6. Do you get anxious when sexual activity is not a part of your daily life?

7. Do you seek sexual partners outside of your marriage or committed relationship?

8. Have you experienced problems in your life as a result of your sexual activities?

9. Do your sexual activities interfere with your normal routine?

10. Do your sexual activities cause health issues for you or your partners?

11. Do you have unprotected sex when you know it's risky?

12. Do your sexual behaviors generate serious consequences for you or others?

The following test can help you assess if you have post-traumatic stress disorder. If you experience some or all of these symptoms, help is available at www.ptsd.va.gov.

1. Have you ever been exposed to a traumatic event that caused you to feel horrified or caused you pain?

2. Did the event involve death or serious injury to someone?

3. Were you in fear for your life or the life of another during the event?

4. Does the event replay in your mind long after the normal grieving process?

5. Do you suffer from nightmares about the event?

6. Do you have difficulty sleeping at night?

7. Do certain things trigger distressing memories about the event?

8. Do you feel intense anxiety when these memories resurface?

9. Do you find yourself doing anything you can to avoid thinking about the event?

10. Does the event come unbidden into your conscious mind to the point that you feel like you are reliving it?

11. Do you find it difficult to share what happened with those close to you?

12. Have you developed an issue with trusting those you once trusted?

13. Is sharing your emotions more difficult than it was before the event?

14. Do you have difficulty with anger, irritability, or concentration since the event?

15. Do you often feel jumpy or startle easily?

16. Have your startle reflexes intensified since the event, and have you become hyper-vigilant?

RESOURCES

A Gift Horse, starring John Schneider

A Hardened Biker Switches Gears, The 700 Club (available on YouTube)

Are You in Need of a Turnaround? A 21-Day Devotional for Men, Ken Paxton

A Strand of Pearls, Theresa Westbrook

Becoming a Man of Valor, Mark R. Laaser

Earl's Pearls, Earl B. Heard

Fighting Back: Living Life Beyond Ourselves, Deena Burnett, Anthony F. Giombetti

Healing the Wounds of Sexual Addiction, Mark R. Laaser

It's What We Do Together That Counts, Earl B. Heard

Louisiana Sports Legends and Heroes—Leaving A Legacy, Earl B. Heard, Dave Moormann

Shattered Vows: Hope and Healing for Women Who Have Been Sexually Betrayed, Debbie Laaser

The Advocates of the Abused and Silent, Theresa Westbrook

The Bible

The Big Book of Alcoholics Anonymous (Including Twelve Steps and Twelve Traditions), Alcoholics Anonymous

The Cry, Kristen Maddox

The Fight of Your Life: Manning Up to the Challenge of Sexual Integrity, Tim Clinton and Mark Laaser

The Will to Survive—A Mental and Emotional Guide for Law Enforcement Professionals and the People Who Love Them, Dr. Bobby Smith, Linda Severson

Turnarounds—A Life of Inspiring Change, Jerry Strickland

Visions of Courage—The Bobby Smith Story, Dr. Bobby Smith

What's in Your Heart Comes Out Your Mouth, Dr. Bobby Smith, Val Penouilh

ACKNOWLEDGMENTS

I would like to thank everyone who revealed your deepest secrets to help us show that there is hope for a wonderful life after hitting rock bottom. Through your experiences, our readers will know without a doubt that faith, hope, and love can conquer anything.

I want to extend a heartfelt thank you to my loving and forgiving wife, Bodi, and to all of you who poured your heart and soul into this project, including Rose Gladner, Susan Mustafa, Tracy Balsz, Steven Scaffidi, New Orleans Mission, Naren Aryal, our BIC Alliance staff, and our BIC Media Solutions team. We also want to give a special thanks to our loyal supporters in business and industry and in our community who helped make this project possible through your kindness and support over the years.

To our families, loved ones, friends, caregivers, and all of you who refuse to give up on those of us at rock bottom even when we have given up on ourselves, thank you. The love and forgiveness you have extended to us when others might have considered those bridges burned have enabled us to love and forgive ourselves.

It is my prayer that you will enjoy and share this inspirational book with anyone you feel may benefit from the pearls of wisdom shared by those who have been to *Rock Bottom and Back*.

May God bless you and your families, and may you always feel His grace as you navigate your way through the maze of life.

Earl B. Heard

Thank you, Earl, for choosing me to write this book. It has truly been an honor to tell these stories. Thank you to everyone featured here for sharing your struggles and triumphs with me. Throughout our interviews, you made me laugh, you made me cry, and you renewed my faith in humanity through your willingness to give of yourselves to make the world a better place.

To my sister Cathy, thank you for staying up late so many nights to offer your editing skills and invaluable advice throughout the writing of this book. To my husband, Scott, thank you for your endless encouragement, support, and love.

And to Rose Gladner, a very special thank you. I could not have accomplished this without you.

Susan Mustafa

ABOUT THE AUTHORS

Susan Mustafa is an award-winning journalist and coauthor of the *New York Times* Best Seller, *The Most Dangerous Animal of All: Searching For My Father and Finding the Zodiac Killer*, written with Gary L. Stewart.

She also coauthored *Dismembered*, the true story of serial killer Sean Vincent Gillis, written with Sue Israel; and *Blood Bath* about the life and crimes of serial killer Derrick Todd Lee, written with Special Prosecutor Tony Clayton and Sue Israel.

Susan has been featured on numerous television programs, which have aired on Discovery, Investigation Discovery, Discovery Canada, Lifetime, and National Geographic.

Susan resides in Baton Rouge, Louisiana, with her husband, Scott.

Earl B. Heard is the founder and CEO of Business and Industry Communications (BIC) Alliance, which includes BIC Media Solutions (BMS)—a custom publishing, event planning, and media investment company. He is also the publisher of *BIC Magazine*, the Western Hemisphere's largest multi-industry energy publication.

In addition to *Rock Bottom and Back*, Earl has published six books through BMS: *It's What We Do Together That Counts, Energy Entrepreneurs, Industry Achievers, Earl's Pearls, Michael Learns to Listen,* and *Louisiana Sports Legends and Heroes—Leaving A Legacy.*

In 2014, BMS expanded its media investments into coproducing and marketing inspirational, faith-based films, including *A Gift Horse*, starring John Schneider. BMS has also produced a companion DVD for *Rock Bottom and Back—From Desperation to Inspiration.*

As an inspirational speaker, Earl shares his wealth of knowledge about how to become successful, both personally and professionally.

Earl resides in Baton Rouge, Louisiana, with his wife, Mary "Bodi" Heard.

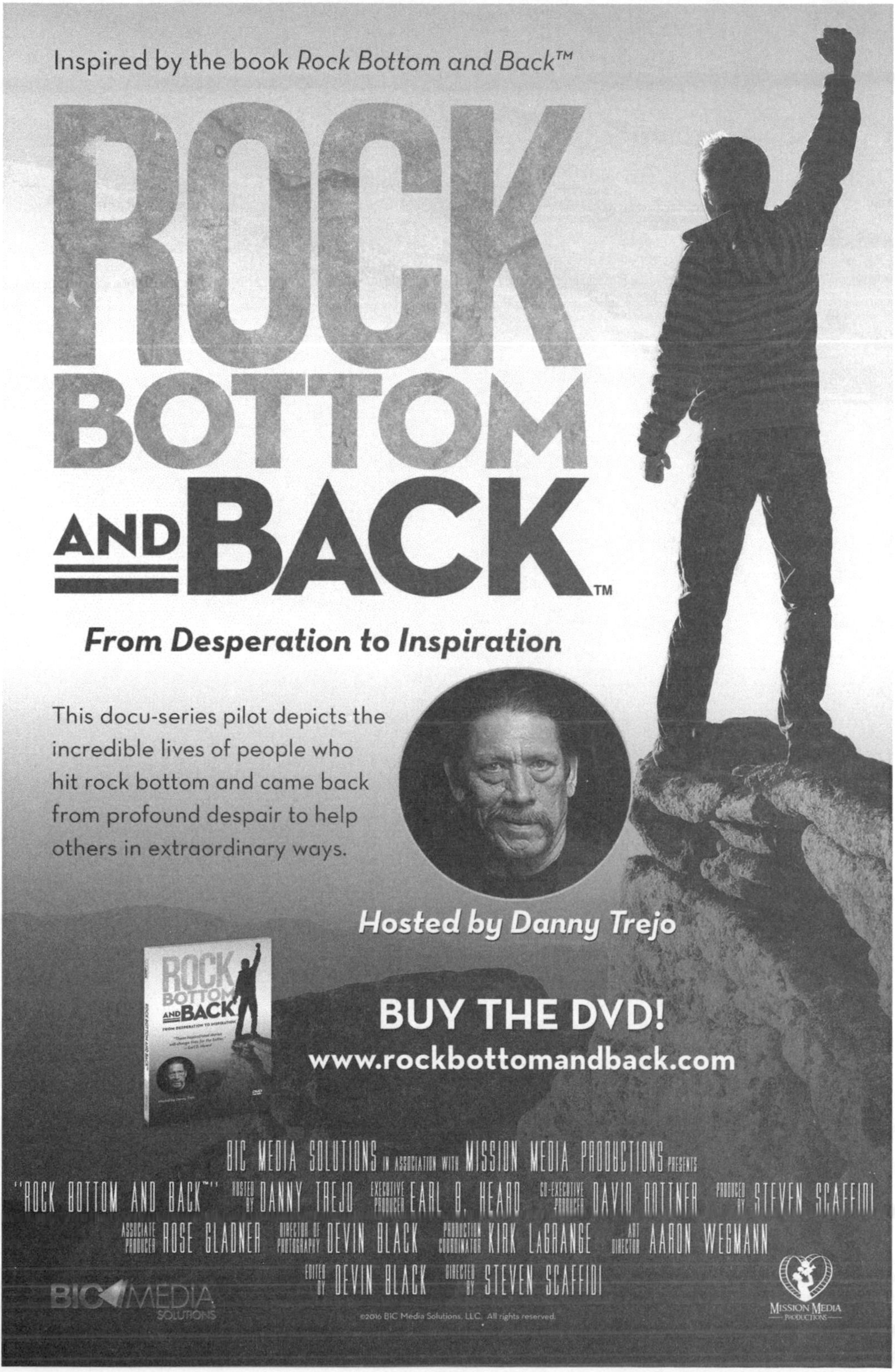

Inspired by the book Rock Bottom and Back™
ROCK BOTTOM AND BACK™
From Desperation to Inspiration
This docu-series pilot depicts the incredible lives of people who hit rock bottom and came back from profound despair to help others in extraordinary ways.
Hosted by Danny Trejo
BUY THE DVD!
www.rockbottomandback.com
BIC MEDIA SOLUTIONS IN ASSOCIATION WITH MISSION MEDIA PRODUCTIONS PRESENTS
"ROCK BOTTOM AND BACK™" HOSTED BY DANNY TREJO EXECUTIVE PRODUCER EARL B. HEARD CO-EXECUTIVE PRODUCER DAVID ROTTNER PRODUCED BY STEVEN SCAFFIDI
ASSOCIATE PRODUCER ROSE GLADNER DIRECTOR OF PHOTOGRAPHY DEVIN BLACK PRODUCTION COORDINATOR KIRK LaGRANGE ART DIRECTOR AARON WEGMANN
EDITED BY DEVIN BLACK DIRECTED BY STEVEN SCAFFIDI
BIC MEDIA SOLUTIONS
©2016 BIC Media Solutions, LLC. All rights reserved.
MISSION MEDIA PRODUCTIONS